ILLINOIS SUPPLEMENT FOR
Modern Real Estate Practice

JOHN D. BALLOU
THOMAS H. BOWMAN, JR.
Consulting Editors

Eighth Edition

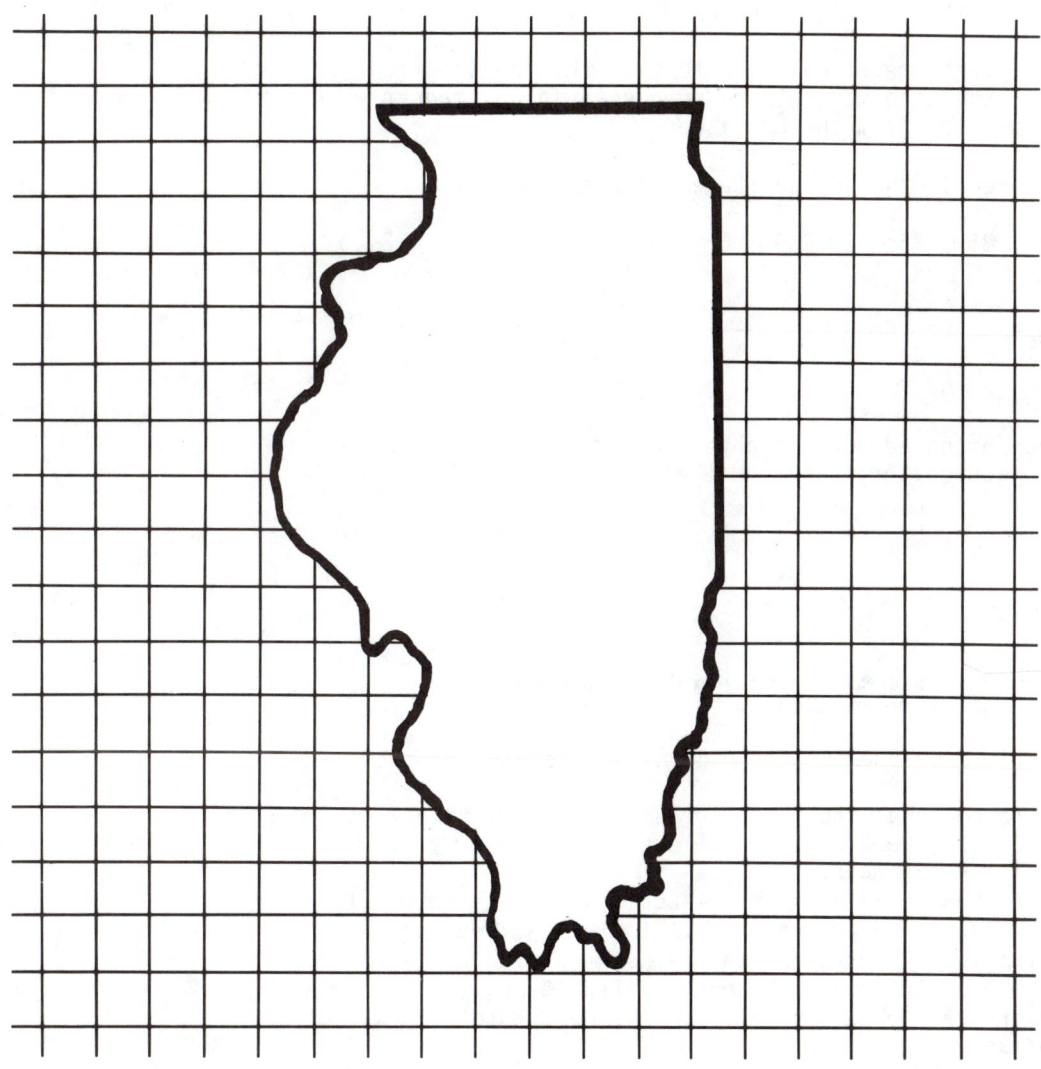

REAL ESTATE EDUCATION COMPANY/CHICAGO
a division of Longman Group USA Inc.

WITH THE ENDORSEMENT OF THE
ILLINOIS ASSOCIATION OF REALTORS

While a great deal of care has been taken to provide accurate and current information, the ideas, suggestions, general principles, and conclusions presented in this book are subject to local, state, and federal laws and regulations, court cases, and any revisions of same. The reader is thus urged to consult legal counsel regarding any points of law -- this publication should not be used as a substitute for competent legal advice.

©1984, 1983, 1978, 1977, 1975, 1973, 1970 by Longman Group USA Inc.

Published by Real Estate Education Company/Chicago,
a division of Longman Group USA Inc.

All rights reserved. The text of this publication, or any part thereof, may not be reproduced in any manner whatsoever without written permission from the publisher.

Printed in the United States of America.

84   85   86   10   9   8   7   6   5   4   3   2

Sponsoring editor: Bobbye Middendorf
Project editor: David Walker

Library of Congress Cataloging in Publication Data
Main entry under title:

Illinois supplement for Modern real estate practice.

   To be used with: Modern real estate practice / Fillmore W. Galaty, Wellington J. Allaway, Robert C. Kyle.
   Includes index.
   1. Real estate business--Law and legislation--Illinois. 2. Vendors and purchasers--Illinois. 3. Real property--Illinois. 4. Real estate business--Illinois. I. Ballou, John D. II. Bowman, Thomas H. III. Galaty, Fillmore W. Modern real estate practice. IV. Real Estate Education Company.
KF2042.R4G34 1982 Suppl. 9   346.77304'37   84-8211
ISBN 0-88462-502-8   347.7306437

Contents

       Preface

5	Real Estate Brokerage	1
6	Listing Agreements	7
7	Interests in Real Estate	11
8	How Ownership Is Held	15
9	Legal Descriptions	23
10	Real Estate Taxes and Other Liens	31
11	Real Estate Contracts	39
12	Transfer of Title	45
13	Title Records	59
14	Real Estate License Laws	65
15	Real Estate Financing	91
16	Leases	97
19/20	Control of Land Use/Subdividing and Property Development	103
21	Fair Housing Laws and Ethical Practices	107
23	Closing the Real Estate Transaction	113
	Appendix: The Real Estate License Examination	127
	Answer Key	145
	Illinois Real Estate License Act	149
	Index	169

The Illinois Supplement and the basic text Modern Real Estate Practice used in combination have proven to be most effective in introducing men and women to the growing complexity of the real estate business. These texts have achieved broad acceptance and respect in college level courses throughout the State and have also established their value in programs to prepare for the Illinois Broker and Salesperson Examinations. With the publication of the updated and expanded 8th Edition of the Illinois Supplement, the Illinois Association of Realtors® is pleased to recommend the continued, widespread use of these texts. The involvement of the Association in endorsing and distributing Modern Real Estate Practice and the Illinois Supplement is a part of the Association's expanded effort to provide quality educational materials and programs to the real estate profession in Illinois.

Illinois Association of Realtors®

Preface

Real estate practice in any state is based upon the state's constitution, laws, regulations and court decisions in addition to fundamental federal laws and regulations. Each state's own legislature, courts and commissions make laws and regulations governing activities in that state.

The Illinois State Legislature meets each January and remains in session until June 30. Thereafter it may be called into special session by order of the governor. In any of these sessions laws may be passed or changes made in existing laws that affect real estate practice.

Also, the practice of real estate in any specific location in Illinois may be influenced by local agencies, bureaus and organizations such as county and city governments or local real estate boards, and by the controls and/or customs that these organizations initiate.

The purpose of this Supplement is to discuss law and operating procedure concerning real estate applicable to the State of Illinois. The Supplement builds on the basic information that is presented in the text Modern Real Estate Practice by Galaty, Allaway and Kyle, also published by Real Estate Education Company, Chicago, Illinois. While every effort has been made not to duplicate the basic information covered in the text, the student should be careful to adapt the information in Modern Real Estate Practice to the special state facts covered in this supplement. Therefore, first study the text lesson and then refer to the same subject area in this Supplement.

The Supplement is closely keyed to the basic text to facilitate easy reference from one to the other. Each chapter number corresponds to that chapter in Modern Real Estate Practice. As you would expect, some chapters in the basic text have no related chapters in this Supplement because the subject involved does not entail law or practice that varies significantly from state to state, e.g., appraisal or property management.

Following each chapter are questions drawn from the material in the text and Supplement. In addition, there is an appendix containing information on the Illinois licensing examination with a practice examination. All questions in this Supplement are similar in format to those that will appear on the Illinois real estate licensing examination.

To enable you to use the questions as both a teaching and testing device, an Answer Key for the questions is included at the end of the book. After completing each chapter, answer the corresponding questions and check your answers with those in the Answer Key. Be certain that you understand each question before proceeding to the next chapter.

John D. Ballou, consulting editor for this Eighth Edition of the Illinois Supplement, is a licensed real estate broker and an attorney at law in private practice in Chicago. Mr. Ballou is a faculty member at Moraine Valley Community College in Palos Hills and an instructor for First United Realtors/Rich Port Realty. He is a member of the American Bar Association, Illinois State Bar Association, and the Chicago Bar Association.

Thomas H. Bowman, Jr., G.R.I., served as consulting editor for the Seventh Edition and reviewer for the present edition. He is an instructor at Triton Community College and an associate broker with Quinlan & Tyson.

Special thanks go to the following reviewers for their thoughtful suggestions: Mary Coveny, First United/Rich Port School of Real Estate; Pat Curtiss, Curtiss Academy of Real Estate, Belleville; and James P. Kane, Jr., Reus/Real Estate Education Company School.

Special assistance has been provided by David Walker, project editor in charge of development, and Jeny Kucenic, acquisitions assistant.

5

Real Estate Brokerage

Principal-Agent Relationship

The principal-agent relationship is described in the text. Some states have laws that require the preparation of a written contract to employ a broker to sell or rent real estate. Illinois has no provision prescribing the complete form of a listing agreement, but current regulations require all exclusive listings to be in writing. Every listing contract must include an automatic expiration date. The person signing this or any other contract must receive a true copy at the time of signing.

Real Estate License Act

Illinois has had a Real Estate License Act since January 1, 1922. The law, administered through the Commissioner of Real Estate under the Illinois Department of Registration and Education, regulates the licensing of brokers and salespeople "for the protection of the public and to evaluate the competency of real estate professionals." The license law is discussed in Chapter 14.

Collecting Commissions

To collect a commission on a real estate transaction, a licensed broker must have a contract of employment, generally known as a listing agreement, in which his or her principal agrees to pay a specified commission. The amount of a broker's commission is a matter to be negotiated between broker and seller. The percentage of commission should be clearly stated in the listing agreement.

In general, the listing broker is entitled to a commission after obtaining a signed contract from a buyer who is "ready, willing and able" to buy on the seller's terms as set forth in the listing. When terms other than those offered by the original listing are agreed upon as indicated by a contract signed by both buyer and seller, the broker is entitled to a commission. In Illinois, the closing of the sale is the usual proof that the broker has produced a buyer and earned a commission.

Salesperson Agreement Required (General Rule VI [A])

Under Illinois law, every broker who employs salespeople, associate brokers, or other brokers, and/or who is associated with other registrants as independent contractors, must have a written agreement with each associate. The agreement must be dated and signed by both parties and should state the responsibilities of each party for such matters as compensation, supervision and duties. As with any contract, changes to any terms of the original written agreement should be in writing, signed, and kept on file. These are subject to examination by the Department, as well as state and federal revenue departments. A copy of the signed agreement should also be given to the associate. The contract may indicate an associate is considered an independent contractor, as defined in the text, for purposes such as federal tax withholding and the broker's potential liability for acts of the associate.

Licensee Liability to Sellers and Buyers

Illinois courts have long held that the contractual principal-agent relationship as defined in the listing contract gives the seller cause for action against the licensee who breaches his or her fiduciary duties to the seller. (See the main text for details.) These same courts, however, have proven very reluctant to find that the licensee owes any fiduciary duty to third parties, including buyers.

Recently, Illinois courts have recognized the rise of consumer protectionism with opinions that appear to mark the decline of the doctrine of caveat emptor (let the buyer beware). Brokers, associate brokers, and salespeople must become aware that they may bear potential liability to buyers via three legal approaches that have figured in recent court decisions.

First, a licensee may be held liable to a buyer when he or she misrepresents material facts about a property and the buyer suffers monetary loss through reliance on these statements. The licensee's loyalty to his or her principal is no defense, even though the principal may have ordered the agent to misrepresent. If the licensee makes statements he or she knows to be untrue, or believes to be untrue, Illinois courts will have no difficulty in finding the licensee liable to the buyer. Furthermore, liability will extend when the licensee is aware of facts that tend to indicate he or she is making a false statement: if the seller tells his or her agent-licensee that "the roof was replaced last year," and the agent has reason to believe that statement to be untrue, the licensee must attempt to ascertain the truth and/or not pass the information on to the buyer.

Second, a licensee may be held liable to a buyer or other third party if the licensee violates the Illinois Real Estate License Act. In the landmark case of Sawyer Realty Group, Inc. v. Jarvis Corporation (1982), the Illinois Supreme Court ruled that there is an implied right of action given to any citizen who suffers dollar damages as a result of a violation of the Act on the part of a licensee. This case did away with the concept that a licensee's duties run only to his or her principal-seller and the State that grants the license privilege.

Third, a licensee may be held liable to the buyer under the Illinois Consumer Fraud and Deceptive Practices Act. Licensees found in violation of this Act may suffer greatly expanded potential liability to third parties. The Illinois Appellate Court has twice ruled on this issue and decided against the licensee. In Beard v. Gress (1980), a broker negligently made misstatements to the buyer regarding the rate of interest on a mortgage encumbering the property and the length of time the property had been on the market. Although the broker's motives were of an innocent nature, the court allowed the buyer relief at common law, stating that the misrepresentations were a deceptive practice since they created "a likelihood of confusion and misunderstanding." Neither the buyer's reliance on the misrepresentations nor the broker's intent to deceive were necessary elements to giving cause of action, according to the court.

In Duhl v. Nash Realty, Inc. (1982), the court again found that an alleged violation of the Consumer Fraud and Deceptive Practices Act provided a cause of action against the agent-licensee. In this case, the seller of a home claimed that his real estate agents had falsely represented that the minimum market value of the home was $158,000. The seller counted on this figure in choosing a new house he purchased through the same agents. At the time the seller sued the agents, the original home was listed with a new broker, and the list price reduced to $137,000, still without a single offer being received. The seller was forced to sell his new house at a loss. The Illinois Appellate Court held that the seller had stated a cause of action against the agent based on a violation of the Act. This case has been remanded to the trial court and had yet to be decided upon its facts as of this printing.

G.R.I Designation

The successful real estate registrant has learned the need for continuing education in real estate. Membership in a Realtors® board and the Illinois Association of Realtors® enables a broker or salesperson to enroll at the Realtors® Institute. A person who is designated a Graduate, Realtors® Institute (G.R.I.), has become known as a person aware of the problems faced in the real estate industry and able to cope with those problems in a professional and ethical manner.

In Illinois, a student is awarded the designation of G.R.I. after successfully completing all three 30-hour courses of the Realtors® Institute and passing final examinations on each course. Certification is limited to persons who hold an active Illinois real estate license, and who are members of the Illinois Association of Realtors® at the time of their graduation from the Institute. A G.R.I. must continue to meet the requirements and standards of the Illinois Association of Realtors® or face loss of the G.R.I. designation.

QUESTIONS

1. An Illinois real estate salesperson who is engaged as an independent contractor:

   a. is considered an employee by the IRS for tax purposes.
   b. must have a written contract with his or her broker.
   c. must be covered by workers' compensation.
   d. may be required to adhere to his or her broker's working hours and dress standards as long as such things are specified in the broker-salesperson contract.

2. In Illinois the usual proof that the listing broker has earned his or her commission is:

    a. the submission to the seller of a signed offer from the buyer.
    b. the closing of the sale.
    c. the signing of an exclusive listing contract.
    d. the deposit of buyer's earnest money into escrow.

3. Broker Al Volari listed the O'Tooles' home for sale at $79,500. The Krauts had contracted with Volari earlier to find them just such a house, agreeing to pay him a commission for this service. The transaction was consummated and Volari was to collect $2,782.50 from the Krauts and $5,565 from the O'Tooles, who did not know about the agreement with the Krauts. Volari can avoid potential liability by:

    a. getting a signed consent form from the Krauts.
    b. informing both the Krauts and O'Tooles at closing.
    c. refusing to accept a commission from the Krauts.
    d. none of the above

4. Broker Sandra Greenberg listed Jay Pierre's home at $60,000. Before the listing contract expired she brought Pierre a full-price offer containing no contingencies not in the listing agreement. Pierre then decided he no longer wanted to sell.

    a. Greenberg has no reason to collect commission in this case.
    b. Pierre is liable for the commission.
    c. Greenberg must immediately file suit against Pierre.
    d. none of the above

5. The law of agency requires a relationship of trust and confidence between principal and agent. This is known as:

    a. a consignment.
    b. a trust accounting.
    c. a fiduciary relationship.
    d. a franchise.

6. Pete the broker tells a prospect that Joe Greene's house has solid oak floors under the carpeting. The other houses in the subdivision have plywood floors. What is Pete's obligation?

    I. to accurately pass on the information Joe Greene gave him.
    II. to tell the prospect that there is reason to doubt that the floors are really solid oak.

    a. I only
    b. II only
    c. both I and II
    d. neither I nor II

7. Geri Bowman is enrolled at the Realtors® Institute. She:

   I. will be certified if she has an active real estate license and is a member of the Illinois Association of Realtors® when she graduates.
   II. must complete three courses of thirty hours each and pass the final examinations to meet the graduation requirement.

   a. I only
   b. II only
   c. both I and II
   d. neither I nor II

8. Salesperson Alan Soline sells John Denver's home to Soline's friend Boston Blackey.

   I. Soline earned a commission when both buyer and seller signed the contract.
   II. Soline should have told Denver that Boston was a friend.

   a. I only
   b. II only
   c. both I and II
   d. neither I nor II

6

Listing Agreements

Listing Agreements (General Rule VII)

In Illinois, all exclusive listing agreements must be written and must include the list price of the property, the amount of the commission and the time it is to be paid, an automatic expiration date for the contract, the names of broker and seller, and the address or legal description of the property. Any changes in the listing that alter the amount of the commission or the time of payment must be in writing and signed by the seller and the broker in order to be valid.

General Rule VII [D] requires that, when a listing includes a provision that the seller will not receive the earnest money deposit if the purchaser defaults, this fact must appear "in letters larger than those generally used in the listing agreement."

Discrimination prohibited. All Illinois listing agreements must clearly state that it is illegal for either the owner or the broker to refuse to sell or show property to any person because of race, color, religion, national origin, sex or physical disability (Rule VII [E]). For a complete discussion of laws and regulations governing discrimination in all phases of a real estate transaction, see Chapter 21.

Automatic expiration date. According to the license law, all listing agreements must contain an automatic expiration date for the contract. A listing agreement without such a provision is void. A registrant is prohibited from including a clause in a listing that automatically extends the listing period (General Rule VII [B]).

Net listings. Although net listings as described in the text are not specifically prohibited in Illinois, such listings are considered undesirable and incompatible with the service nature of the brokerage business.

Guaranteed sales. Guaranteed sale agreements given as part of the inducements to acquire a listing must be given in writing and are subject to additional requirements. See Chapter 14.

Disclosure of Material Facts

General Rule V requires a registered broker or salesperson to reveal all material facts concerning a property to any purchaser, prospective purchaser,

8 ILLINOIS SUPPLEMENT for Modern Real Estate Practice

seller, lessee, lessor or any party to the transaction as soon as it is practical to do so. Material facts are any facts upon which a reasonable person would base his or her decision. However, the rule respects the fiduciary relationship between broker and principal by stating that a registrant is not required "to violate his duties under the laws of agency."

This rule further requires the registrant to disclose in writing to all parties in any transaction any direct or indirect interest he or she has as owner, purchaser, seller, renter, or lessor of the real estate involved.

<u>Disclosure of special compensation</u>. The registrant is also prohibited from accepting "any finder fee, commission, discount, kickback, or other compensation from any financial institution, title insurance company, or person other than another registrant" unless he or she discloses the receipt of these fees in writing to all parties to the transaction.

<u>QUESTIONS</u>

1. Illinois salespeople may:

    (a) take a net listing as long as it is in their broker's name.
    b. refuse to show a property to racial minorities if their sellers so instruct them.
    c. advertise in their name as long as they hold independent contractor status.
    d. none of the above

2. In addition to the names of broker and seller and the address or legal description of the property, all exclusive listings must contain:

    a. an automatic expiration date.
    b. the list price of the property.
    c. the amount and time of payment of the commission.
    (d) all of the above

3. In Illinois, an exclusive listing contract:

    a. can include a clause that automatically extends the listing for three months.
    b. must contain an automatic expiration date.
    c. must be in writing.
    (d) b and c

4. Jose LaPaloma has secured a listing on John Johnson's condominium. Johnson then sold the unit to his brother-in-law. LaPaloma was still entitled to a commission. This is an example of a:

    a. net listing.
    b. multiple listing.
    (c) exclusive-right-to-sell listing.
    d. exclusive agency listing.

5. Bill Blass listed the Givencys' home. The listing contract included a clause providing for an original term of 120 days, with an automatic extension thereafter until terminated by either Blass's or the Givencys' written notice. This contract:

   a. is valid if the home is sold within the first 120 days.
   b. is void.
   c. is valid if the home is sold at any time for full list price.
   d. both a and c are true

6. The Owings house was listed at $74,500, so the couple anticipated a minimum net of $67,500. They actually netted $67,680 after paying a 6 percent commission but before closing costs were deducted. What was the selling price?

   a. $70,387
   b. $70,500
   c. $71,740
   d. $72,000

$X = $ Selling Price

$94\% \text{ of } Y = 67680$

7

Interests in Real Estate

ESTATES IN LAND

Estates in land (also referred to as ownership interests) are set forth for each state including Illinois in the chart included in Chapter 7 of the text. Also included in this chart are forms of real estate ownership that are discussed in detail in Chapter 8 of the text and the Illinois Supplement.

Government Powers

All four government powers described in the text are held by the State of Illinois. The Illinois law regarding escheat, however, provides that when a property owner dies intestate (without a will) and leaves no ascertainable heirs, his or her real estate escheats to the county in which it is located—not to the state.

Prescriptive Easements

As noted in the text, prescriptive easements are established by the extended use of land without the owner's permission. In Illinois this use must be adverse, exclusive, under claim of right, and continuous and uninterrupted for 20 years before a prescriptive easement can be created. Private owners of pedestrian walkways in shopping centers and large commercial and industrial buildings have prevented the public from acquiring prescriptive easements by blocking public access for one 24-hour period in each calendar year. However, Illinois law now allows owners to prevent the establishment of such easements by posting signs along the boundary lines of the property which state that access is by permission of the owner.

Dower

As of January 1, 1972, the inchoate right of dower was abolished in Illinois. No spouse has a right of dower in the owning spouse's real estate. Consequently, curtesy does not exist in Illinois.

Homestead Exemption

An estate of homestead is given by Illinois law to every householder with a family who occupies land and buildings as a residence. The homestead is presently exempt from claims of unsecured creditors to the extent of $15,000. This exemption continues after the death of the householder for the benefit of the surviving spouse as long as he or she occupies the homestead and for the benefit of children under 21 years of age as long as they occupy the homestead. Generally, no notice has to be filed or recorded to establish or reveal a homestead. (See Chapter 10 for a more detailed discussion of tax benefits for senior citizens.)

Since homestead rights are not recorded, prospective buyers, lienholders and other concerned parties are charged with inspecting the premises to see if the occupant can claim homestead rights. (See Chapter 13 of the text for an explanation of actual vs. constructive notice.)

Homestead rights are released or waived by a conveyance in writing signed by the owner and his or her spouse or the survivor (see Chapter 12). The signatures of both spouses are needed on listings, sales contracts, conveyances, and mortgages to release possible homestead rights, even if the property in question is owned solely by either the husband or the wife.

QUESTIONS

1. In Illinois, homestead exemptions:

    a. must be recorded with the county recorder.
    b. are limited to $15,000.
    c. can never be released.
    d. all of the above

2. A conveyance of real estate by a married person must also be executed by the married person's spouse:

    a. to release homestead rights.
    b. only if the property is owned by both parties.
    c. to release dower rights.
    d. all of the above

3. In Illinois, a prescriptive easement:

    a. may be established by 20 years of continuous and uninterrupted use without the owner's approval.
    b. may be prevented by blocking access for one 24-hour period each calendar year.
    c. may be prevented by posting signs stating that access is by permission of the owner.
    d. all of the above

4. In Illinois, when real estate of a decedent escheats:

    a. the heirs must be compensated for its fair market value.
    b. the laws of eminent domain apply.
    c. the property goes to the county in which it is located.
    d. the property is exempt from claims of creditors up to $15,000.

5. James Evans died and by his will gave his lakefront cottage to his wife for her use as long as she lives, with the provision that title shall pass equally to their children upon her death. The widow Evans holds:

    a. a fee simple estate.
    b. an estate at will.
    c. a life estate.
    d. a determinable fee estate.

6. The Stumps bought a home immediately behind the Fallons. The survey the Stumps ordered indicated the Fallon's chain link fence had been placed 18 inches onto the Stump's lot. This is an example of:

    a. adverse possession.
    b. an encroachment.
    c. an easement appurtenant.
    d. an easement by necessity.

7. Esther Silverman made a gift of a house she owned to her daughter Ruth for her lifetime, with a provision that the real estate will pass to her granddaughter Sandra after Ruth's death. Sandra holds:

    a. an estate for years.
    b. a life estate.
    c. a reversionary interest.
    d. a remainder interest.

8. At the time of the gift described in the above question, Sandra's interest in the real estate:

    a. is a future interest.
    b. may never be effective.
    c. is a conditional interest.
    d. is none, until Ruth dies.

9. Apartment house owner Paul Rifkin has given Sue Stewart in 2B the right to use a designated area of ground this summer for a garden. Sue holds:

    a. a personal easement in gross.
    b. an easement appurtenant.
    c. a license.
    d. a prescriptive interest.

8

How Ownership Is Held

FORMS OF OWNERSHIP

The form of ownership in which a title is held is determined by the purchaser. Any owner may change this form of ownership at any time as long as he or she owns the property. Illinois recognizes ownership in severalty and two kinds of co-ownership: joint tenancy and tenancy in common.

Joint Tenancy

A joint tenancy is created when real estate is transferred to two or more co-owners by one deed of conveyance that expressly states or contains language that clearly indicates that the grantees are acquiring title as joint tenants. The right of survivorship is a distinct feature of joint tenancy, and all co-owners own an equal indivisible share.

Tenancy in Common

A tenancy in common is created when real estate is transferred to two or more co-owners by a deed or deeds of conveyance that may state nothing concerning the character of the tenancy to be acquired. Under such deeds, the grantees are said to acquire title as tenants in common.

A single deed may show the proportional interests of each tenant in common, or separate deeds issued to each tenant may show that tenant's individual proportional interest. When a single deed is used, lack of a description of each tenant's share means all holders own equal undivided shares.

Interests of tenants in common are passed to the heirs of a deceased holder of record unless the deceased's will provides otherwise.

Note that real estate conveyed to "A and B, husband and wife" creates a tenancy in common. In order to create joint tenancy the deed must convey to "A and B, husband and wife, as joint tenants."

Illinois provides that an owner (or owners) may execute a deed to themselves and others "as joint tenants and not as tenants in common" and thereby create a valid joint tenancy without using an intermediary or nominee (or "straw man") as required under "the four unities" practice (see text). Therefore, the unity of time is not required in Illinois to create a joint tenancy.

In 1983, the Illinois Supreme Court held that a joint tenant may sever the tenancy by conveying his or her interest as a joint tenant to him- or herself as a tenant-in-common. This decision also recognizes the nonessential nature of the "straw man."

Partition. Every co-owner of real estate in Illinois has a right of partition. He or she may file a suit to divide the property regardless of whether title is held in joint tenancy or tenancy in common. A partition suit may be filed by one or more of the owners in the Circuit Court of the county in which the parcel of land is located. The court appoints from one to three commissioners who must, if possible, make a division of the property among the owners in title. However, if such division cannot be made without prejudice to the rights of the co-owners, the commissioners must report to the court the valuation of the property. The property is then offered for public sale for not less than two-thirds of the value as set by the commissioners. All parties to the suit are required to pay their proportionate share of court costs and the attorney's fees of the plaintiff. Upon completion of the sale, confirmation of the sale by the court and delivery of a proper conveyance to the purchaser at the sale, the proceeds of the sale are then delivered to the sellers according to the court order.

Partnerships

The Illinois Legislature enacted the Uniform Partnership Act in 1917. The act includes provisions that permit title to real estate to be acquired, held, and conveyed in the partnership name. Due to the involved nature of partnership matters, legal counsel should always be consulted.

Corporations

Since corporations are legal entities and are treated as fictitious persons, they may own and transfer real estate just as if they were people. A corporation generally acquires ownership in severalty, but may hold property as a co-tenant with other corporations and/or people. The creation of corporations, and their regulation, is controlled by the Illinois Business Corporation Act of 1983.

Trusts

Illinois permits title to real estate to be held in trusts as described in the text. Real estate may be held in trust as part of a living or testamentary trust or as the sole asset in a land trust.

Land Trusts

Land trusts are extensively used in Illinois. Title to the real estate is conveyed to the trustee by a Deed in Trust, which confers upon the trustee much the same powers to deal with the real estate as any individual owner could. (See the Forms Appendix in the text for sample Deed in Trust.) Upon recording the Deed in Trust, the powers vested in the trustee can be relied upon by disinterested third parties as having been properly established.

The beneficiary of a land trust is almost always the settlor (trustor), i.e. the person who establishes the trust. The role of the trustee is defined by the trust agreement executed between the trustee and the settlor. The typical land trust agreement gives the beneficiary full power of management and control.

Twenty-year time limits are customarily used in land trust agreements. However, the time limit may be extended if the beneficiaries sign an extension agreement. Under another provision of the usual land trust agreement, if the beneficiaries are not available, the trustee may resign and execute and record a deed conveying the title to the beneficiaries. If the trust agreement is not extended or the trustee does not resign, the usual land trust agreement provides that the trustee shall sell the real estate at a public sale after giving reasonable notice and distribute the net sale proceeds to the beneficiaries of this trust.

Legally, the interest of the beneficiary is personal property, not real estate. It consists of the right to the income from the property and to the proceeds of any sale. Since the beneficiary no longer owns the real estate, a judgment against the beneficiary does not create a lien against the real estate in which he or she holds a beneficial interest. If the beneficiary dies without a will, his or her interest in the trust is distributed to the heirs in a different manner than if it were real estate. (See Chapter 12, Laws of Descent.)

The land trustee does not normally disclose the name of the beneficiary without the beneficiary's written authority, but may be forced to do so under certain circumstances, including receipt of a proper demand and notice from the Internal Revenue Service. Illinois law now requires the trustee to disclose the beneficiary's name to the concerned housing authority within ten days after receiving a complaint of a violation of a building ordinance or law. The trustee must also reveal the beneficiary's name when applying to any State of Illinois agency for a license or permit affecting the entrusted real estate.

Land trusts are used for a variety of reasons:

1. Involuntary, statutory, and judgment liens that affect the beneficiary's real estate will not attach to property held in a land trust (except tax liens);

2. Because the public records show the trustee as owner, a person can assemble large tracts of property for development without the public becoming aware of the process and causing a rise in the area's real estate prices;

3. Transferability is much simpler since deeds and mortgages are not required--the transfer can be made simply by assigning the beneficial interest;

4. Beneficial interests are not subject to marital rights or homestead rights, so only one spouse may convey the property held in a land trust;

5. Beneficial interests may be pledged as collateral for loans without the elaborate procedures of the typical mortgage/note transaction;

6. Partnerships are greatly benefitted by placing their real estate in a land trust because doing so insulates the general partners' interests from the usual unlimited liability; and

7. Partition suits are not available to dissident co-beneficiaries, so multiple owners are protected from frivolous litigation.

Condominiums

The Condominium Property Act was established in Illinois on July 1, 1963. Under this act, an owner may elect to submit a parcel of real estate to condominium ownership by recording a "declaration" to which is attached a three-dimensional plat of survey of the parcel showing the location and size of all units in the building. A building built on leased land may not be submitted for condominium ownership in Illinois. Every unit purchaser acquires the fee simple title to that unit, together with the percentage of ownership of the common elements which is set forth in the declaration and which belongs to that unit. This percentage is computed on the basis of the initial list prices of each unit. An example of a legal description of a condominium unit follows:

> Unit No. _____ as delineated on survey of the following described parcel of real estate (hereinafter referred to as "Development Parcel"): Lot 1 in Charles A. Nixon's Consolidation, in Section 27, Township 42 North, Range 13 East of the Third Principal Meridian, in Cook County, Illinois, which survey is attached as Exhibit "A" to declaration made by 1420 Corporation recorded in the Office of the Recorder of Cook County, Illinois, as Document No. 2094195 together with an undivided ____% interest in the common elements as set forth in said declaration and survey.
>
> Grantor also hereby grants to Grantee(s), their successors and assigns, as rights and easements appurtenant to the above described real estate, the rights and easements for the benefit of said property set forth in the aforementioned Declaration, and Grantor reserves to itself, its successors and assigns, the rights and easements set forth in said Declaration for the benefit of the remaining property described therein.
>
> This Condominium Deed is subject to all rights, easements, restrictions, conditions, covenants and reservations contained in said Declaration the same as though the provisions of said Declaration were recited and stipulated at length herein.

The survey required with each declaration of condominium ownership must indicate the dimensions of each unit. This survey will show the outlines of the lot, the size and shape of each apartment and the elevation or height above base datum for the "upper surface of floor level" and its "lower surface of ceiling level." The difference between these two levels represents the air space owned in fee simple by the unit owner.

Real estate taxes are assessed against each unit, including its corresponding percentage of the common elements. Such tax bills are usually sent to the unit owners.

The owner's association. When a certain percentage of the units in a new condominium property are sold by the developer, the condominium owners form a unit owners' association, which is usually incorporated as a nonprofit corporation. The association members elect a Board of Directors to act as the legal unit for operating the property, as a whole. The Board is usually required to obtain fire and extended coverage insurance on the property for full replacement cost, provide for the maintenance of common elements, and perform any other actions entrusted to them by the association. Assessments of common expenses for insurance and other operating costs are to be collected by the Board from all unit owners. Unpaid assessments become a lien on the unit assessed and the Board may foreclose such lien in the same manner as a mortgage.

At any time, the property may be removed from the Act by the unanimous consent of all owners and all lienholders, as evidenced by a recorded written instrument. All owners would then be tenants in common. Condominium unit owners have no individual rights of partition.

If a building is damaged by fire, the insurance proceeds, if sufficient, must be used for reconstruction. If such insurance is insufficient and unit owners do not voluntarily provide for the reconstruction of the building, then a notice removing the property from the Condominium Act as described above may be prepared and recorded.

QUESTIONS

1. Al Crenshaw owned his Peoria residence when he and Marge were married. Afterward he executed and recorded a deed to himself and Marge as joint tenants. Two months later Al put his interest in a land trust. As a result:

    a. Marge and the trust now own the property as tenants in common.
    b. Al and Marge now own the property as tenants in common.
    c. Al still owns the property in severalty because it is not legal in Illinois to create a joint tenancy in this manner.
    d. none of the above

2. The names of the beneficiaries of a land trust must be revealed by the trustee:

    a. to the Internal Revenue Service.
    b. within ten days after receiving a written complaint of violation of a building ordinance or law.
    c. to a person purchasing the property held by the trust.
    d. a and b

3. Every co-owner of real estate in Illinois has the right to file a suit for partition when:

    a. the property is held in joint tenancy or tenancy in common.
    b. the property is held in a land trust.
    c. the property is owned as a condominium.
    d. all of the above

4. Agnes McGinty has been named trustee of an Illinois land trust. The following is true:

    a. Agnes is the owner of all the real estate held in the trust.
    b. Agnes now has full control over the management and disposition of the real estate held in the trust.
    c. The beneficiaries' interest in this trust is considered personal property. A notice of this interest, however, must be recorded in order to be valid when the property is transferred.
    d. all of the above

5. The owner of a condominium apartment holds:

    a. a fee simple title to the space that comprises the unit as described in the declaration.
    b. a percentage of the common elements of the building and grounds as shown by the survey attached to the declaration.
    c. a percentage of recreational facilities, such as clubhouse, tennis courts, or golf course, when ownership is included in the development.
    d. all of the above

6. Title to land in Illinois may be held and conveyed:

    a. in the name of a partnership.
    b. as joint tenants only if owned by husband and wife.
    c. as tenants in common with rights of survivorship.
    d. all of the above

7. If the deed of conveyance to Illinois land transfers title to two or more co-owners without defining the character of the co-ownership:

    a. the property is held in joint tenancy.
    b. the co-owners are tenants in common.
    c. the deed is invalid.
    d. the co-owners have the right of survivorship.

8. The Collingsworths have just purchased a cooperative apartment. Which of the following is true?

    a. They will receive a conditional fee title to their apartment at closing.
    b. They will be assessed annually for taxes on their unit and the corresponding percentage of the common elements.
    c. They will have a voice in the management of their apartment building and grounds.
    d. all of the above

9. An apartment building may be put under condominium ownership by:

   a. the owner recording a condominium declaration with a three-dimensional plat.
   b. the recording of a certificate stating that a majority of all tenants cast a favorable vote.
   c. the election of a board of directors, having the power to act as legal administrator for the property.
   d. all of the above

10. Cathy Carbow bought a condominium in Handsome Manor. Indicate whether:

    I. she will contribute her proportional share of taxes assessed the association so they may be paid on time.
    II. she owns her unit in severalty.

    a. I only
    b. II only
    c. both I and II
    d. neither I nor II

11. The purpose of the land trust agreement is:

    a. to enable the trustee to control the property.
    b. to enable the beneficiary to control the property.
    c. to prevent the beneficiary from selling the property.
    d. a and c

12. By a deed of conveyance, title to Illinois land is transferred to "Robert and Dolores Frame, husband and wife." They now own the property as:

    a. joint tenants.
    b. tenants in common.
    c. tenants by the entirety.
    d. a homestead exemption.

13. The form of ownership in which a fee simple title will be held is decided by:

    a. the title insurance company that issues the owner's title insurance policy.
    b. the mortgage firm that makes the first mortgage loan.
    c. the owners at any time during their ownership.
    d. the purchasers before they sign a purchase contract, as it cannot be changed after the closing of the sale.

14. Bill and Delores Dallesandro own their home in joint tenancy. When Bill died, his will provided for half of his estate to go to Delores and the remainder to be divided equally among their four surviving children. Now:

   I. Delores owns 50 percent interest in the home.
   II. each child holds a 1/8th interest as tenants in common.

   a. I only
   b. II only
   c. both I and II
   d. neither I nor II

9

Legal Descriptions

Rectangular Survey System

As federal surveyors moved across the country they chose certain reference points to use in constructing base lines (east-west) and meridians (north-south), which would be used to define large areas of land. Under the Federal Rectangular Survey System, properties within each area would be defined in terms of a particular base line and meridian. Locations in Illinois are described by their relationship to one of the three meridians shown on the map on the next page.

The Second Principal Meridian is located in Indiana and controls that portion of Illinois lying south and east of Kankakee. The Third Principal Meridian begins at Cairo, at the junction of the Ohio and Mississippi Rivers, and extends northward through Centralia and near Rockford to the Illinois-Wisconsin state line. The Fourth Principal Meridian begins near Beardstown and extends northward to the Canadian border. Surveys of land located in the western portion of Illinois use a base line for the Fourth Principal Meridian at Beardstown. Surveys of land in Wisconsin and eastern Minnesota are made from the Fourth Principal Meridian using a base line which is the Illinois-Wisconsin state line.

Because some areas have odd shapes, not all property is defined by the nearest reference line. Looking at the Illinois map on the next page, you will see that a property on the western border of the Third Principal Meridian and just west of Rockford will nevertheless be described by reference to the Fourth P.M. There are no options with regard to the meridians and base lines used to describe a particular property: once made, a description will not change.

Metes and Bounds Descriptions

As indicated in the text, metes and bounds descriptions are used in Illinois when describing irregular tracts, portions of a recorded lot or fractions of a section. Such descriptions always refer to the section, township, range and principal meridian of the land.

24 ILLINOIS SUPPLEMENT for Modern Real Estate Practice

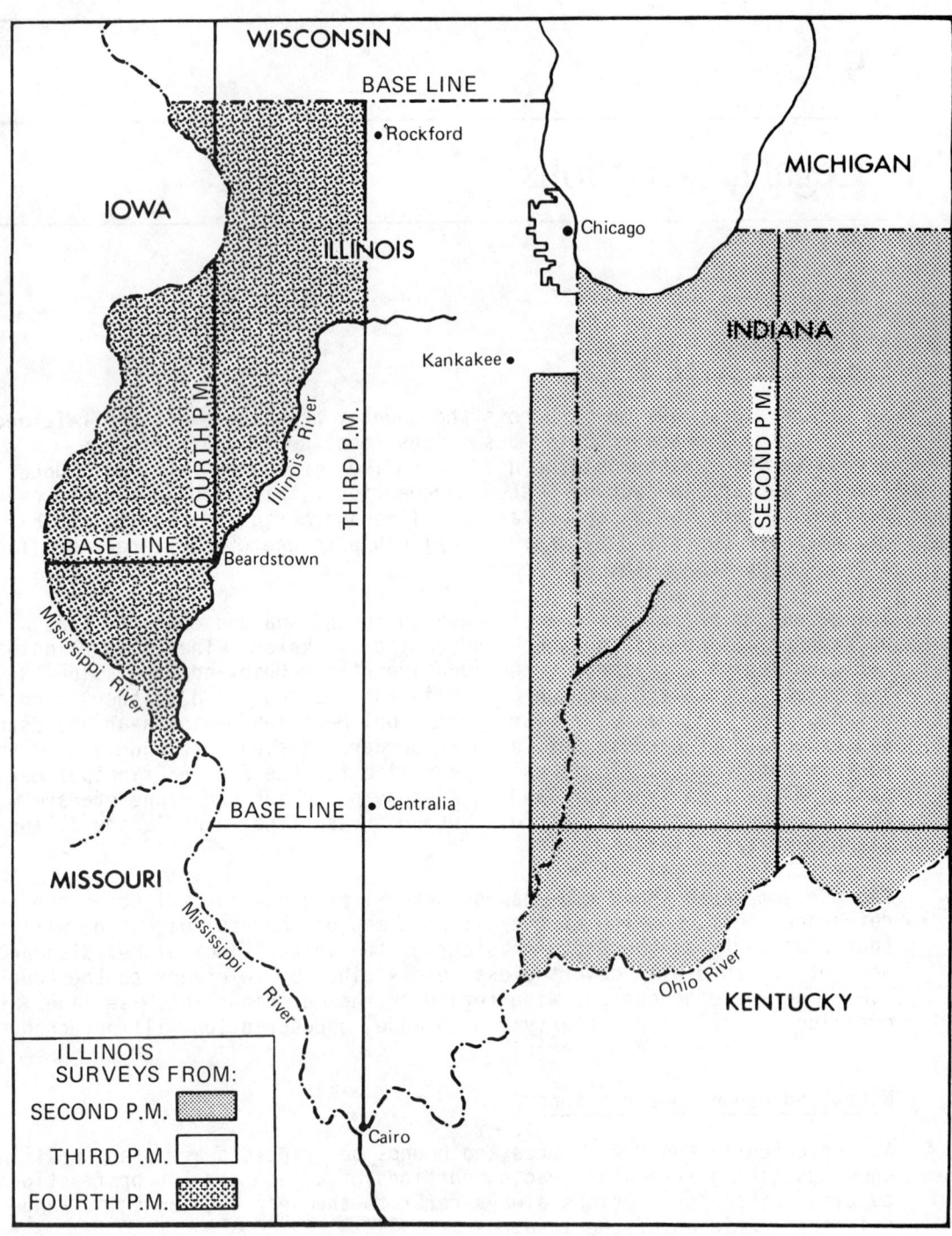

9/Legal Descriptions 25

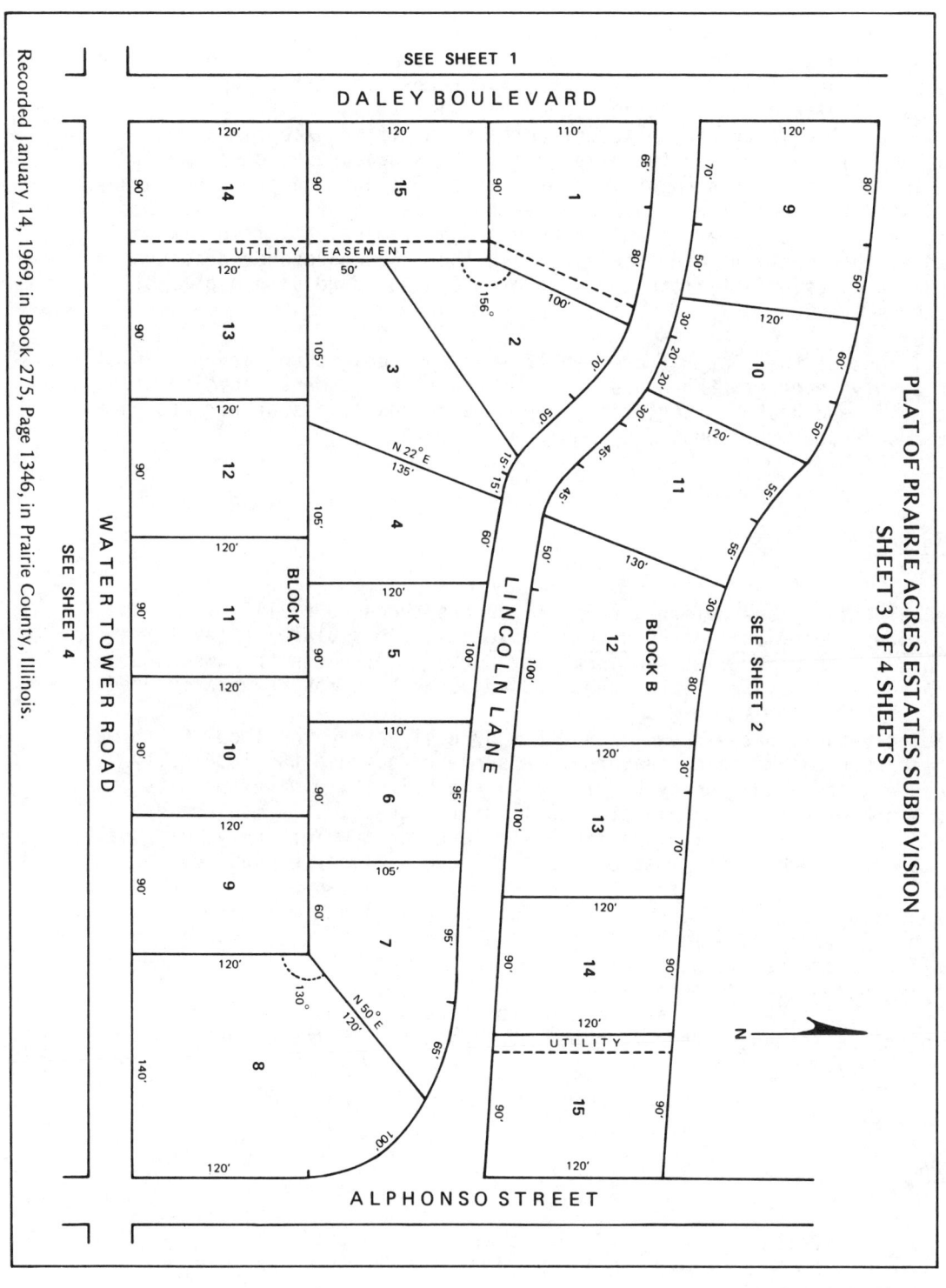

Plat Act

Under the Illinois Plat Act, when an owner divides a parcel of land into two or more parts, any of which is less than five acres, the parts must be surveyed and a plat of subdivision recorded. Page 25 shows part of such a plat description. There are, however, certain specified exceptions in the Plat Act dispensing with the need to meet this statutory requirement. An example would be the division of lots or blocks of less than one acre in any recorded subdivision that does not involve the creation of any new streets or easements of access. However, when a conveyance is made, an affidavit may be required by the county recorder to establish that the conveyance does not constitute a division into lots the size of which would require a plat of survey to be made.

The provisions of the Plat Act are complicated and subject to interpretation by each county recorder. When preparing to record a document conveying land under a metes and bounds description, one should consult his or her attorney and the county recorder about the requirements to be met.

ILLINOIS DATUM

The general datum plane referred to by surveyors throughout Illinois is the United States Geological Survey datum (U.S.G.S.). This plane or level is based upon mean sea level at New York City Harbor. Although this measurement has been adjusted several times, the 1929 adjustment is most generally used.

Some cities establish their own city datum by designating the local bench mark from which such datum can be measured. A surveyor can use the local city datum or indicate elevation by reference to the U.S.G.S. These two sets of figures expressing the same elevation will differ greatly. A measurement based on the U.S.G.S. datum plane (mean sea level at New York City) is usually a much larger figure, since most U.S. cities have a higher elevation.

From the Chicago City Datum, other reference points (bench marks) were established in various permanent locations throughout the city. These were given official status by the Department of Public Works by being assigned identifying numbers. The purpose of this was to simplify the work of surveyors in that they could select a nearby bench mark as a base for determining elevations, rather than having to begin from the mother bench mark for each survey.

QUESTIONS

1. Legal descriptions of land in Illinois are based upon:

   a. the Rectangular Survey System.
   b. The Third, Fourth, and Fifth Principal Meridians.
   c. a single base line running through the central part of the state.
   d. all of the above

9/Legal Descriptions   27

2. Elevations of land or heights of buildings in Illinois:

    a. are generally based on the mean sea level of New York City Harbor.
    b. may vary in accordance with the local datum used in the survey.
    c. are used in the legal descriptions of condominium properties.
    d. all of the above

3. Richard Gamble has a ten-acre tract of land that he wants to divide into four 2 1/2-acre lots and sell for residences. He must:

    a. establish a datum for the area.
    b. have a spot survey made of the proposed lots.
    c. record a copy of the plat before offering lots for sale.
    d. all of the above

4. Compute the number of acres in the NW1/4 of the NE1/4 of section 16. Then multiply that answer by the number of miles around the township where section 16 is located. The result is:

    a. 960.
    b. 1440.
    c. 2880.
    d. 5760.

5. Land in the northwest corner of Illinois is surveyed from which Principal Meridian?

    a. Second
    b. Third
    c. Fourth
    d. Fifth

6. If Tom Flock buys a new home in Vista Ridge, a subdivision located in the Village of Arlington Heights:

    I. his land will be surveyed by the rectangular survey system.
    II. his home is probably described by lot number on a recorded plat.

    a. I only   c. both I and II
    b. II only   d. neither I nor II

28   ILLINOIS SUPPLEMENT for Modern Real Estate Practice

7. A parcel of land is described as: "All that part of lots 9 and 10 in Homeowner's Pleasant Acre subdivision in sections 5 and 6, T39N, R14E of the Third P.M. in Cook County, Illinois, described as follows: beginning at the NE corner of lot 6, thence southward along the east line of lot 6, 174 1/2 feet thence westward parallel with the south lines of lots 5 and 6, 315 feet, thence northward parallel with the west line of lot 6 to the north line of lot 5, thence eastwardly along the north lines of lots 5 and 6 to the place of beginning." This is called a description by:

   a. the Rectangular Survey System.
   b. metes and bounds.
   c. recorded subdivision plat.
   d. all of the above

8. Sheldon Kosinsky wants to put a two-strand barbed wire fence around the NE1/4, section 31, T5N, R3E of the Fourth Principal Meridian. Barbed wire fencing comes in 80-rod rolls that cost $46 each. Exclusive of posts, gates, and labor, how much will this fencing cost Kosinsky?

   a. $132
   b. $368
   c. $736
   d. $1,472

9. Which of the following dimensions equal one acre?

   a. 1/640th of a section
   b. 43,560 square feet
   c. 90' x 484'
   d. all of the above

Answer questions 10 through 14 using the information given on the plat of Prairie Acres Estates on page 25.

10. Which of the following statements is true?

   a. Lot 9, block A is larger than lot 12 in the same block.
   b. The plat for the lots on the southerly side of Water Tower Road between Daley Boulevard and Alphonso Street is found on sheet 3.
   c. Lot 13, block B is larger than lot 14 in the same block.
   d. Lot 14, block A is in the SE corner of sheet 3.

11. Which of the following lots has the most frontage on Lincoln Lane?

   a. lot 10, block B
   b. lot 11, block B
   c. lot 1, block A
   d. lot 8, block A

12. "Beginning at the intersection of the east line of Daley Boulevard and the south line of Lincoln Lane and running south along the east line of Daley Boulevard a distance of 230 feet; thence easterly parallel to the north line of Water Tower Road a distance of 195 feet; thence northeasterly on a course of N22°E a distance of 135 feet; and thence northwesterly along the south line of Lincoln Lane to the point of beginning." Which lots are described here?

    a. lots 13, 14, and 15, block A
    b. lots 9, 10, and 11, block B
    c. lots 1, 2, 3, and 15, block A
    d. lots 7, 8, and 9, block A

13. On the plat, how many lots have easements?

    a. two
    b. three
    c. four
    d. five

14. Assuming a 20-foot setback from Water Tower Road and a 10-foot setback from all other lot lines, what is the total buildable area in lot 9, block A?

    a. 5400 square feet
    b. 6300 square feet
    c. 7000 square feet
    d. 8000 square feet

10

Real Estate Taxes and Other Liens

GENERAL REAL ESTATE TAXES

In Illinois, general taxes are levied annually for the calendar year and become a specific lien on January 1 of that tax year. However, they are not payable until the following year.

General taxes are based on three components:

1. The <u>assessed value</u> of each parcel of real estate being taxed.

2. The applicable <u>equalization factor</u> expressed as a decimal.

3. The <u>tax rate</u> generally expressed in cents or dollars per $100 of assessed valuation.

Illinois law requires county assessors to recompute assessed valuation quadrennially. All assessments are published in full in a newspaper of general circulation serving the area of the property, and a written notice is sent to the taxpayer of record. The assessor may adjust the assessed value yearly on those parcels whose use has changed during the year. Furthermore, the assessed valuation of all real estate is adjusted yearly in each county by applying an equalization factor determined by the Property Tax Administration Bureau of the Department of Revenue. The equalization factor is designed to counteract discrepancies in the assessments in the various counties so that all Illinois citizens will pay taxes at the same rate. For example: two similar three-bedroom homes were sold for $90,000 each. One was assessed in County A for $40,000 and the other was assessed in County B for $20,000. The examination of the signed transfer tax declarations revealed that the average assessed valuations for similar properties was $30,000. So County A was assigned a 0.7500 equalization factor and County B was assigned a factor of 1.5000.

To calculate the tax due, the assessed valuation is multiplied by the equalization factor. Both houses in the example then have an equalized assessed value of $30,000. If the tax rate is $3.50 per $100 of valuation, the homeowners will be assessed $1,050 in general real estate taxes. (Calculation for house in County A: $40,000 assessed valuation times 0.7500 equalization factor equals $30,000 equalized assessed valuation; $30,000 divided by 100 equals 300 one-hundred-dollar units; 300 times a tax rate of $3.50 gives a tax of $1,050.)

The assessor has the responsibility to distinguish real property from personal property. The State Supreme Court ruled that after 1978, personal property cannot be assessed for tax purposes.

The owner of the property may contest the value placed on the property by the assessor. The taxpayer should first file a complaint in the assessor's office. A further appeal can be filed with the Board of Appeals, which has the authority to review and change any disputed assessment.

Taxes are levied by each separate taxing body such as the village, county, school district, sanitary district, park district, and so forth. From the assessor's records of valuation, each taxing body determines the total assessed value of all land and improvements within its taxable jurisdiction. Based on the taxing body's budget for operations for the given year, and after revenue available from other sources is determined, the taxing rate required to raise the needed money from tax on real estate can be computed. While taxes are levied by each taxing body, only one tax bill is prepared by the County Collector each year.

Many counties, including Cook, use a system of permanent tax numbers to identify real estate for tax purposes. This system makes it necessary for an owner, before paying his or her tax, to be sure that the permanent tax number shown on the tax bill is the number assigned to the legal description of the property.

Should real estate taxes be paid on the wrong parcel of real estate, it is the responsibility of the payer to try to collect from the true lot owner. Tax officials are not charged with the duty to correct such a mistake.

Homestead Property Tax Exemptions

In Illinois, taxes are adjusted to reflect certain concessions given on properties in which owners reside. These properties are designated as homesteads. The Homestead Exemption reduces the assessed value of a property subject to taxes.

Property owners may qualify for this concession on the basis of _age_, _physical disability_, _increase in the assessed value of the taxable property_, or _improvements to the property_.

Age. Owner occupants may reduce the equalized value on their primary residence by up to $2,000 if they are 65 years of age or older. Renters do not qualify unless they own and live in taxable residential homes built upon rented land (a leasehold of land).

Physical disability. Homes of disabled veterans used exclusively by them or an unremarried surviving spouse are entitled to a reduction of $30,000 from the assessed valuation. This is for housing specifically adapted to a veteran's disability as authorized by Title 38, Chapter 21 of the U.S. Code.

Increase in assessed value. A residential homeowner may deduct an amount equal to the increase in the equalized assessed value of the residential property above the equalized assessed value of 1977, up to a maximum exemption of $3,500. The County Assessor, Supervisor of Assessments, or Board of Assessors determines the eligibility of property to receive the exemption.

Improvements. Properties with new improvements to existing structures qualify when owned and used exclusively for a residential purpose. The exemption is limited to the actual value of the improvement up to an annual maximum of $25,000 and continues for four years.

Multiple residential property having fewer than 55 units may qualify for improvements worth up to an annual maximum of $30,000 actual value per unit. The property must be used primarily for residential purposes, but need not be owner-occupied. The exemption period also continues for four years from the date the improvement is completed. The building must be at least 30 years old and the improvement must be designed to improve its condition or energy efficiency. A certificate must be filed with the Recorder/Registrar of Deeds agreeing to restrictions and showing evidence that the property's increase in assessed value is due only to the improvements. During the exemption period the property may be used only for residential purposes and not be converted to condominiums.

Other exemptions. Additional exemptions that may be used to reduce taxes on Illinois property include a homestead maintenance and repair exemption, a solar heating exemption, and an airport land exemption.

Additional Senior Citizen Benefits

Homeowners or renters 65 years of age and over may, if qualified, receive a check for a portion of their property taxes or rent. The entitlement comes from The Senior Citizens and Disabled Persons Property Tax and Rental Relief Act (commonly referred to as The Circuit Breaker). The Department of Revenue, State of Illinois, provides the forms and administers the act.

The amount of the check depends on the applicant's total annual household income in the taxed year and the amount of the tax bill. Total income includes all gross income of both spouses, including social security, pensions, dividends, and all interest. The total must not exceed $12,000. For renters, 30 percent of the rent paid during the year is considered the property tax. The grant amounts to the tax paid, less three and one-half percent of the household income, up to a maximum of $700 less five percent of the household income.

Under the "Additional Tax Relief Program," senior citizens may apply for an additional grant of up to $80 as relief from other types of taxes.

Due Dates

General taxes are payable in two equal installments in the year after they are levied: one-half by June 1 and the second half by September 1. These payment dates are called penalty dates after which a 1 1/2 percent-per-month penalty is added to any amount unpaid. Since bills must be issued 30 days prior to a penalty date, the penalty date for an installment may be delayed if the County Collector is late in preparing the bills. Penalty dates of March 1 and August 1 have been authorized for Cook County taxes under an accelerated billing procedure. With this accelerated procedure, the billing for the installment due by March 1 is sent before the actual tax has been determined. The amount of this first accelerated installment is one-half of the amount of the tax bill for the previous year. The second installment, due by August 1, is billed after the tax has been determined and is for the actual tax, less the amount billed as the first installment. Several other county boards have now adopted the accelerated billing system.

Tax Sales

If the tax has not been paid on a property, a tax sale may be held by the county after the due date of the second installment. Sales in some counties are held in October; in other counties they are held later.

Bidders at a tax sale must pay the full amount of the outstanding taxes. They bid on the rate of interest they will accept when the owner redeems the property by paying the taxes plus interest. The bidder who quotes the lowest rate of interest becomes the successful purchaser.

Redemption. Real estate sold for delinquent taxes may be redeemed by the owner or persons with legal interests (except undisclosed beneficiaries of a land trust). However, after the tax sale, the county continues to add large penalty amounts to the unpaid tax. Therefore, if redemption is made, payment must include the delinquent taxes, any interest due the tax sale purchaser, and all penalty amounts added before and after the tax sale. Payment is made to the county clerk in the form of cash, cashier's check, certified check, or postal or bank money order.

The time period allowed for redemption varies depending on the nature of property involved. Vacant non-farm real estate, commercial or industrial property, or property improved with seven or more residential units must be redeemed within six months from date of sale. Other real property may be redeemed anytime within two years. Properties with six or less units, where the taxpayer owner resides, have a two-and-a-half-year redemption period.

If the property is not redeemed by the owner within the period allowed and the tax sale purchaser desires to establish ownership of the property, he or she is required to give notice to the delinquent owner and certain others with interest in the property. Then he or she can apply for a tax deed. However, the tax sale purchaser must pay the taxes on the property for each year subsequent to the tax sale and until he or she has secured a tax deed. A tax deed must be recorded within one year after the expiration of the redemption period or it becomes null and void.

Scavenger sale. Property subject to delinquent taxes and not sold at the annual tax sale is forfeited to the state and the penalty is added to the unpaid taxes at the rate of 18 percent per annum. Title to these forfeited properties may be acquired by submitting a bid to the state for a specific property under so-called scavenger sale provisions. These bids are for the purchase price that the bidder is willing to pay the state for the property. Owners of record still retain statutory redemption rights over the highest bidder, but they must pay the state all past-due taxes and penalties in order to redeem. Successful nonowner bidders need not pay past-due taxes and penalties to take title.

Mobile Homes

In Illinois, a mobile home is classified as personal property rather than real estate because it is not permanently affixed to the ground on which it rests. If a mobile home in Illinois can be shown to be immobile, and thus permanently attached to the ground on which it rests, the tax assessor may decide that it is real property.

Special Assessments

Special assessments apply in Illinois as described in the text. These assessments may be levied on nearby property as well as the property to be improved on the theory that the neighboring property stands to benefit from the improvements. The annual due date for assessment payments in Illinois is generally January 2.

Special assessments are payable in annual installments, generally over a period of ten years. Interest is charged annually on the outstanding unpaid balance. Property owners generally have the right to prepay installments or the entire outstanding balance to stop interest charges.

Mechanic's Lien

A mechanic's lien is a statutory lien that attaches to the improved property. To be enforceable, the statutory requirements must be followed explicitly. Legal counsel should be consulted. The rights vary between general contractors, subcontractors, and material suppliers. The following is intended to give the student only a general understanding of this very technical and legal right of lien.

In order for builders or others who improve real estate by providing labor or material to be able to claim a mechanic's lien, they must be able to show that they were hired by the landowner or an authorized agent. In Illinois, if the landowner knew of the work ordered or being done, but did not object or disclaim responsibility for payment, then this is considered sufficient to create a mechanic's lien.

A builder who constructed a building on the wrong lot would have difficulty enforcing a mechanic's lien unless the owner of the improved lot knew of the work and did not object to the completion.

In Illinois, general contractors whose bills have not been paid and who wish to enforce their lien rights (against the mortgagee [lender], other lienholders, and any subsequent purchasers) must file their lien notices with the County Recorder within four months after the work is completed. The filing deadline for subcontractors working on a large construction job is within four months after completion of their particular work. Subcontractors have the right in Illinois to file for their unpaid claim even though the general contractor has been paid in full. The lien takes effect as of the date when the work was ordered or the contract signed by the owner. From the point of view of the public or a prospective purchaser, an unpaid contractor has a secret lien until the lien notice is recorded.

The contractor's lien right will expire two years after completion of that contractor's work unless he or she files suit within that time to foreclose the lien. This suit will force the sale of the real estate through a court order to provide funds to pay the claimant's lien.

The names of all subcontractors must be listed by the general contractor in the "Sworn Statement," which is presented to the landowner who ordered the work. "Waivers of Lien" are collected from each contractor, subcontractor, and material supplier (materialman) as payments are made for work done. In this way, the owner's attorney or a title insurance company can check to determine if all possible lienors have released their lien rights.

Judgments

Judgments resulting from court suits or a confession under a judgment clause in a note, lease, and so forth become a general lien on all the debtor's real and personal property in a county when the judgment is recorded in the County Recorder's office or entered on the Torrens title records by the Registrar of Titles. By recording a memorandum of judgment in another county, the lien also becomes effective in that county. Such liens are effective for seven years and may be renewed for another seven-year term.

QUESTIONS

1. The equalization factor used in Illinois taxation is designed to:

    a. increase the tax revenues of the state.
    b. correct discrepancies between the assessed value of similar parcels of land in various counties.
    c. correct inequities in taxes for senior citizens and disabled persons.
    d. all of the above

2. Homeowner Carl Norris contracted with the Belding Construction Company to add a bedroom to his house on June 17, 1983. The work was completed by August 28, 1983, but Mr. Norris still had not paid for the work by November 28. The Belding Company records a mechanic's lien against the property. The lien:

    a. takes effect as of June 17.
    b. takes effect as of August 28.
    c. takes effect as of November 28.
    d. may not be recorded more than two months after the work is completed.

10/Real Estate Taxes and Other Liens   37

3. Bob Swindle owns a condominium townhouse in Cook County and a weekend retreat in Lake County, Illinois. He also owns investment property in Colorado. If one of his creditors sues him in a Cook County court and a judgment is issued against him and is recorded in Cook County, which of the following is true?

   a. The judgment becomes a lien on the townhouse, Swindle's two cars and other items of personal property in Cook County.
   b. The judgment becomes a lien on the weekend retreat, speedboat, and all other items of real and personal property in Lake and Cook counties.
   c. The judgment becomes a lien on all of Swindle's real and personal property.
   d. The judgment becomes a lien on the townhouse only.

4. The successful bidder on property offered at a tax sale:

   a. owns the property after he or she pays the outstanding taxes.
   b. bids the lowest percentage of interest he or she will accept if the property is redeemed.
   c. may obtain a tax deed if the property is not redeemed within the redemption period.
   d. b and c above

5. With an accelerated billing procedure, such as that used in Cook County, the first installment of the tax bill:

   a. is computed on the previous year's taxes.
   b. is due on April 1.
   c. includes special assessments for the current year.
   d. none of the above

6. Senior citizens in Illinois:

   a. must have a combined annual income of less than $12,000 to apply for a Tax Relief Act benefit.
   b. are entitled to a reduction in the assessed value of their owner-occupied residences.
   c. may receive a property tax relief check from the state if they qualify.
   d. all of the above

7. Pfaff owns two lots and hires Contractor Ventolo to build a house on one of them. Ventolo builds Pfaff's house on the wrong lot. Can Ventolo enforce a mechanic's lien if Pfaff fails to pay him?

   a. Yes, if Ventolo can prove that Pfaff knew of the work done.
   b. Yes, if Ventolo can prove that Pfaff did not object to the completion of the work.
   c. Yes, if Ventolo can get the support of his subcontractors.
   d. a and b above

38   ILLINOIS SUPPLEMENT for Modern Real Estate Practice

8. Special assessments:

   a. may be levied only on property that is improved.
   b. are payable in monthly installments with interest charged each month on the unpaid balance.
   c. are payable in annual installments with interest charged annually on the unpaid balance
   d. may not be prepaid.

9. Potts bought an apartment building for $325,000. At the time of purchase, it had a fair market value of $350,000. It has an assessed value of $94,500. The equalization factor is 1.1000. The basis on which the general real estate tax is computed is:

   a. $94,500.
   b. $325,000.
   c. $350,000.
   d. none of the above

10. The Brooks own a home valued at $80,000 that is assessed for tax purposes at 25 percent of market value. The equalization factor for the county in which the residence is located is 1.5000 and the tax rate is $6 per hundred. The first half of the real estate tax would be:

    a. $720.
    b. $900.
    c. $1,200.
    d. $1,800.

11. What happens if Samantha F. receives a tax bill with an index number different from the one shown on her title policy?

    I. She must make sure which is correct.
    II. The assessor becomes responsible for the unpaid bill.

       a. I only   c. both I and II
       b. II only   d. neither I nor II

11

Real Estate Contracts

THE REAL ESTATE SALES CONTRACT

Many forms of real estate sales contracts are used in Illinois. Most of these forms are available in standardized, printed copies that provide many alternative provisions to be used or ruled out by the broker depending on the requirements of the parties.

General Rule VII [A] of the License Act prohibits the registrant from requesting that a contract or document be signed if it contains blank spaces that are to be filled in later.

Once the contract is signed, the broker cannot make any addition, deletion, or alteration in the document without the written or telegraphic consent of all persons who signed the original contract. When the authorized changes are made, they must be signed or initialed by all original signers (General Rule VIII [B]).

When preparing a sales contract, a broker or salesperson is prohibited from changing the commission payment terms designated in the listing agreement unless the seller and broker have agreed to the changes in a separate, signed, written memorandum (General Rule VII [C]). For example, broker Martin has worked very hard to secure a buyer for George Beam's house within two weeks and both Martin and Beam agree that, because of his prompt results, the broker is entitled to a larger commission than the 6 percent provided by the listing agreement. The two parties must prepare and sign a memorandum stating their intention to raise the commission rate from the 6 percent provided in the listing contract to the agreed 6 1/2 percent.

All registrants are required to give each person signing or initialing an original contract a "true copy" of the document at the time of signing (General Rule VIII [C]).

Offer-to-Purchase Forms

In Illinois, a registrant is not permitted to use any form designated "Offer-to-Purchase" when the form will be used as a binding real estate contract. Any real estate contract that will be binding on the parties must state this fact in a large, bold heading (General Rule VIII [D]).

Statute of Frauds

The Illinois Statute of Frauds requires that contracts for the sale of land and all contracts, including leases that will not be fulfilled within one year from the date of making, must be in writing to be enforceable in court. (See Supplement Chapter 16 for a complete discussion of leases.) All written contracts must be signed either by the parties bound by the contract or by some other person authorized in writing by such parties to sign for them. Furthermore, real estate contracts used by registrants must bear notice in large lettering that the contract is legally binding.

Destruction of the Premises

Illinois is a state that has adopted the Uniform Vendor and Purchaser Risk Act as described in the text. Thus, a seller in Illinois must bear any loss that occurs from the time the sales contract is signed by both buyer and seller until the title is transferred or until the buyer takes possession, whichever occurs first.

Earnest Money Escrow Rules

Under General Rule IV, all brokers must establish special accounts for the deposit of all earnest money and other funds entrusted to them in connection with real estate transactions. Each broker must maintain a complete ledger of all earnest money transactions, and notify the Department of Registration and Education of the name of the bank where the money is deposited. All such funds must be deposited to that account no later than the next business day following the acceptance of the real estate contract. This account must be noninterest-bearing unless the broker is directed otherwise in writing by both the buyer and seller, with accrued interest going to the buyer. The social security number of beneficiaries of an interest-bearing account must be reported to government taxing bodies.

The rule requires brokers to make a complete record of all escrow account activity. Only the broker or an authorized agent may withdraw funds from such an account. The broker or broker-salesperson must review, sign, and assume full responsibility for every closing statement prepared by him or her, or by salespeople acting under the broker's supervision and control. Fees earned by the broker from the funds in this account are to be withdrawn by the next day after the transaction is terminated or consummated, or by agreement with the principals. Both the account and the records are subject to inspection at any time by the Department.

Legal Age

In Illinois, the law now provides that all persons become of legal age upon reaching their 18th birthday and thereafter may make and be held legally liable for contracts. Contracts entered into by minors in Illinois are voidable until they reach majority and for a reasonable time thereafter. There is no statutory period within which a person may avoid a contract after reaching majority. What is considered "reasonable" depends on circumstances, and courts tend to allow a maximum of six months. Contracts made by a minor for what the law terms necessaries are generally enforceable. Necessaries include such items as food, clothing, and shelter. While a real estate sales contract with a minor would probably not be enforceable in Illinois, leases or rental agreements signed by minors are generally enforceable, since short-term housing is generally considered a necessary.

Holiday Transactions

A deed or contract executed on a Sunday or legal holiday is valid and enforceable in Illinois. However, when the last day on which a deed or contract must be executed is a holiday or Sunday, such deed or contract may be executed on the next business day.

Personal Property Listed in Real Estate Sales Contracts

It is usual to include in the sale of residences some articles of personal property such as drapes, carpeting and refrigerators, as well as items that are undoubtedly fixtures, such as screens and storm windows. It is now customary in Illinois for all such fixtures and/or chattels (items of personal property) to be listed specifically in the sales contract. This eliminates possible arguments over which items are fixtures and which are chattels, and which chattels are to be included and excluded. Although items of personal property are listed in the sales agreement, title to personal property is usually transferred by a bill of sale. Real estate contract forms used in Illinois normally provide for the inclusion of personal property.

Farm Property

In selling farm property, consideration must be given to the disposition of the annual crops. These crops may be corn, oats, wheat and similar annuals, or fruits or berries growing on trees or bushes that are part of the real estate. It is customary when Illinois farmland is sold for possession to be transferred to the buyer on March 1, which is normally after the last year's crops have been harvested and before the new crops are planted. Usually, then, no special provisions are required regarding the annual crops. However, when possession is transferred to the buyer on March 1, it is also customary for the buyer to assume full payment of the current year's tax bill without proration to date of sale, since he or she will get the full benefit of the new crop for that tax year.

If the sale is closed at other times during the year and before the crops are harvested, the sales contract should provide whether or not the growing crops are included in the sale price. Sometimes when the crop is included in the sale the buyer reimburses the seller for out-of-pocket costs of the crop already incurred including seed, planting, fertilizing and spraying.

Installment Contract Sales of Real Estate

Among the provisions of Illinois law governing the installment contract sale of a dwelling structure are the following:

The law declares void any provision in a contract or agreement made after January 1, 1968, which (1) forbids the contract buyer to record the contract, (2) provides that recording shall not constitute notice, or (3) provides any penalty for recording.

In Illinois, any installment contract for the sale of a dwelling is voidable at the option of the buyer unless there is attached to the contract or incorporated therein a certificate of compliance or an express warranty that no notice from any city, village, or other governmental authority of a building code violation has been received within the past ten years. If any notice has been received within the past ten years, any and all such notices (if not complied with) must be listed with a detailed explanation. Neither buyer nor seller may waive this requirement.

If a buyer, under an installment contract, purchases residential property containing six units or less from a land trust, he or she must be told the names of all beneficiaries of the trust at the time the contract is executed. The buyer has the option of avoiding the contract if the names are not revealed. When an installment contract is involved in a real estate transaction, legal counsel should be consulted.

Limitations on Brokers' Contract-making Authority

Under a 1966 Illinois Supreme Court ruling in the case of the Chicago Bar Association, et al. v. Quinlan and Tyson, a real estate broker is authorized to fill in the blanks in a printed form of a sales contract that is customarily in use in the community where the broker does business and to supply factual information so that a contract may be prepared for signature by buyer and seller. A real estate broker is prohibited from preparing or completing any document necessary to carry out or implement the contract; e.g. deeds, bills of sale, affidavits of title, notes, mortgages, etc. To do so has been ruled as "practicing law," and only attorneys are licensed to practice law; that is, to give legal advice and prepare documents that determine the rights of the parties.

This limitation on the broker's activity also places a responsibility on the broker. When the printed forms do not adequately cover a particular situation, he or she should recommend that buyer and seller have their attorneys meet to prepare an adequate sales contract. Brokers who are also attorneys must decide whether they wish to act as brokers or attorneys, since they cannot be both in a single transaction.

One form of real estate sales contract used in Illinois that complies with the court ruling is reproduced in Chapter 11 of the text. This has been completed by filling in the blanks to represent a sales transaction.

QUESTIONS

1. The statute of frauds requires which of the following contracts to be in writing?

    a. a real estate sales contract
    b. a two-year installment contract for a purchase of a refrigerator
    c. a six-month apartment lease
    d. a and b above

2. In preparing a sales contract an Illinois broker may:

   a. fill in factual and business details in the blank spaces of a customary preprinted form.
   b. prepare and attach original riders to alter a preprinted contract to fit the transaction.
   c. execute an offer to purchase.
   d. a and b above

3. On Tuesday, broker Ben Sharp received an earnest money deposit from Ned Bascomes. The seller accepted the sales contract on Thursday. Sharp must:

   a. keep complete records of the receipt and deposit of the funds.
   b. deposit the money in his special checking account by Friday of that week.
   c. deposit the money in his special trust account by Wednesday of that week.
   d. a and b above

4. An Illinois broker must have written consent of both parties to a transaction to:

   a. deposit earnest money in an interest-bearing account.
   b. fill in the blanks on a sales contract.
   c. make changes in the terms of a signed sales contract.
   d. a and c above

5. Broker Snively obtained a listing agreement from Widow Weed under duress. The contract is:

   a. valid.
   b. void.
   c. voidable.
   d. illegal.

6. After the sales contract has been signed, the broker must:

   a. record the contract to comply with the provisions of the Illinois Statute of Frauds.
   b. have the legality of the contract verified by his or her attorney.
   c. deliver a true copy of the contract to each person signing the original contract.
   d. all of the above

7. A person in Illinois who purchases property under an installment contract:

   a. has the right to have the contract recorded.
   b. may void the contract unless it includes a warranty that any notices of building code violations received within the last ten years have been corrected.
   c. has an interest in the real estate known as equitable title.
   d. all of the above

8. Sixteen-year-old Mike Bowman earned enough money by selling secondhand junk to buy a piece of real estate, on which he planted pumpkins. Which statement(s) describe(s) legal consequences?

    a. Nine months after he turns 18 he asks for his money back and the seller must return it to him.
    b. When the seller learns that Mike was 16, he refuses to give possession because there was not a good contract.
    c. Nine months after harvesting and selling the first pumpkin crop, Mike can ask for all his money back and return possession to the seller.
    d. all of the above

9. When Geri Holden was presented with a contract from Pat Wood, a prospective buyer, it was acceptable in all respects except the closing and possession dates. What can be done?

    I. If she signs the contract as presented, it is enforceable.
    II. The contract can be changed after signing if both buyer and seller agree and sign a rider that explains the changes.

    a. I only
    b. II only
    c. both I and II
    d. neither I nor II

10. Kline paid French $150 for the right to lease a desirable commercial property at any time within 60 days at a stipulated annual rental. Such an agreement is termed an:

    a. open lease.
    b. option.
    c. implied contract.
    d. assignment.

11. Failure to fulfill one's obligation under a valid contract is called a:

    a. delinquency.
    b. defect.
    c. breach.
    d. fault.

12. The Cutters sold their home to the Shears. The deed was executed and delivered on Sunday, May 1, in Rockford, Illinois. Which of the following is true?

    a. The deed is invalid.
    b. The deed is unenforceable.
    c. The deed should have been executed and delivered on Saturday, April 30.
    d. The deed is valid.

12

Transfer of Title

LAW OF DESCENT

The Illinois Law of Descent and Distribution provides that real estate located in Illinois owned by a deceased resident or nonresident who did not leave a valid will is distributed as indicated by the following brief digest of the provisions of the law:

1. If the deceased left one or more children or descendants of children and a surviving spouse, the surviving spouse takes one-half of each parcel of real estate. The child, children or descendants of deceased children share the remaining one-half.

2. If the deceased left a surviving spouse but no children or descendants of children, the surviving spouse takes all the real estate.

3. If there is no surviving spouse and the deceased left one or more children, the children take the estate equally among themselves, unless there are descendants of a deceased child, in which case such descendants take the share their deceased parent would have received if living.

4. If there is no spouse or descendants, then the real estate is divided among parents, brothers and sisters. If one parent is dead, the surviving parent takes two shares; descendants of deceased brothers or sisters take their share by representation--they receive equal portions of their parent's share.

5. If there are no surviving heirs, provisions are made for finding heirs by tracing back through maternal and paternal grandparents and great grandparents.

6. If a decendent left no surviving spouse and no kindred or heirs, the real estate escheats to the county in which the land is located.

Dower rights, and therefore curtesy, in Illinois real estate were abolished effective January 1, 1972 (see Chapter 7).

Debts, if any, and inheritance taxes of a deceased person must be paid out of the estate before the estate is given to the heirs or devisees.

WILLS

Illinois law regarding wills provides that any person of age 18 or more, being of sound mind and memory, make a will. A will must be in writing and signed and declared by the maker (the testator) to be his or her last will and testament in the presence of two or more witnesses. Witnesses should not be persons receiving gifts under terms of the will.

Upon the death of a testator who owns real estate, his or her will is filed for probate in the circuit court of the county where the decedent resided. The executor is appointed and the decendent's assets are inventoried. Claims may be presented to the executor for debts owed by the deceased. Payment of approved claims, inheritance, and estate taxes is made and the remaining assets are distributed. Upon completion of probate, the executor's final account is filed with the court and the executor is discharged. Thereafter, the real estate is considered free from debts, claims, or taxes of the decedent.

A surviving spouse may not be disinherited by the decedent spouse. The surviving spouse is given a statutory right to renounce the will and then to claim as follows:

1. if the deceased left no child or descendant(s) of a child, one-half of the personal estate and one-half of each parcel of real estate.

2. if the deceased left descendants, one-third of the personal estate and one-third of each parcel of real estate.

When a spouse renounces the will and takes his or her statutory share provided by the Law of Descent, the will remains operative with respect to the balance of the estate, but any and all provisions in favor of the renouncing spouse are inoperative.

ADVERSE POSSESSION

Adverse possession of real estate for 20 years defeats legal title to real estate in Illinois. Adverse possession for seven years with a claim and color of title plus payment of taxes can also result in title to the extent of the title shown by the public records. Legal title by adverse possession should not be relied on without legal advice. Usually a court proceeding is required to perfect such title.

DEEDS

The following are the minimum requirements for a valid deed in Illinois between grantor and grantee:

1. the name and signature of the grantor;
2. the name of the grantee;
3. the words of conveyance; and

4. an adequate description of the property.

If the property is the homestead of the grantor, the deed must be signed by both the grantor and spouse to release the spouse's homestead rights.

Illinois deeds must be signed by the owner (grantor), and the owner's marital status must appear in the deed. Homestead property is not identifiable by reading a deed or from examining the public records. Because of the difficulty in determining whether a property is a homestead, if the grantor is married the deed will undoubtedly require the signature of the spouse to release possible homestead rights.

To make a deed recordable, the names of the grantors must be typed or printed below their signatures, and the grantee's address must be stated in the deed.

The main text mentions that some states require grantors to sign under seal. At common law, a seal was a wax impression. Today, to seal generally means to write the initials L.S. after a signature. Illinois does not require seals for individual grantors' signatures, but corporations must affix their corporate seal when they are grantors.

The notary acknowledgment is accepted as proof of execution by the grantor. Such acknowledgment is not necessary to the validity of the deed, nor to enable it to be recorded. However, title insurance companies usually require notary acknowledgment of deeds covered by title insurance policies.

Warranty Deeds

Illinois law provides that a deed using the words "convey and warrant" includes all covenants of general warranty, which are as binding on the grantor, his or her heirs and personal representatives as if written at length in the deed. Such warranties are listed in the law as: (1) possession of a fee simple estate with power to convey, (2) title free from all encumbrances, except those listed in the deed, and (3) quiet and peaceable possession with defense of the title against all claims questioning the grantor's ownership.

Grant, Bargain, and Sale Deeds

In Illinois, a deed using the words "grant, bargain and sell" conveys a fee simple title with the following covenants: (1) grantor holds a fee simple estate, (2) the premises are free from encumbrances made by the grantor, and (3) grantor and his or her heirs and assignees warrant quiet enjoyment. Note that this bargain and sale deed includes warranties not found in the general bargain and sale deed discussed in the text.

Quitclaim Deeds

A quitclaim deed using the words "convey and quit claim" conveys in fee all existing legal and equitable rights of the grantor, if any, held at the time of delivering such deed.

48   ILLINOIS SUPPLEMENT for Modern Real Estate Practice

ILLINOIS STATE AND COUNTY TRANSFER TAX

The Illinois Real Estate Transfer Tax Act became effective January 1, 1968. The tax is computed at the rate of 50 cents for each $500 or fraction thereof of taxable consideration. When the real estate is transferred "subject to" an existing mortgage made by the seller before the time of transfer, the amount of the mortgage remaining unpaid is deducted from the full consideration to determine the taxable consideration.

The tax must be paid at the time of recording of the deed, by purchase of transfer tax stamps from the County Recorder of the county in which the deed is to be recorded. Stamps may be affixed to the deed either before or after recording. Recording is defined to include filing under the Torrens Act. The proceeds of the transfer tax are divided equally between the county and the State of Illinois.

The amount of consideration (value) used for determining the tax must be shown on the form entitled "Real Estate Transfer Declaration," also known as the "Green Sheet." This form, reproduced on pages 50-53, must be signed by the buyer and the seller or their agents. The form provides details of the property description, the manner of conveyance, and the financing used. The financial data helps the Department of Revenue to more accurately determine equalization factors between different counties, and to eliminate inconsistencies caused by the use of nonconventional "creative" financing.

The complete Green Sheet must accompany every deed presented to the Recorder for recording. A willful falsification or omission of any of the required data constitutes a Class B misdemeanor punishable by up to six months in jail. The information contained on the form is not confidential and is available for inspection by the public.

Certain deeds are exempted from the tax, such as those conveying real estate from or between any governmental bodies; by charitable, religious or educational institutions; securing debts, releasing property as security for a debt, partitions, tax deeds, deeds pursuant to mergers of corporations, deeds from subsidiary to parent corporations for cancellation of stock and deeds subject to federal documentary stamp tax. When the actual consideration for conveyance is less than $100, the transfer is exempt from tax. An Exemption Statement is usually typed on an exempted deed and signed before the deed is recorded.

Tax Formula

The formula used in Illinois to determine the taxable consideration is as follows:

Full actual consideration (sale price) $_____
Less amount of personal property included in purchase price $_____
Less amount of mortgage to which property remains subject $_____
Equals net taxable consideration to be covered by stamps $_____
Amount of tax stamps (50 cents per $500 or part thereof
of net taxable consideration) $_____

Rules for Transfer Tax Stamp Calculation

The following summary of rules should help you to work out stamp tax problems based on Illinois tax requirements:

1. There is no tax required if the total actual consideration is less than $100. Such deeds usually bear a notation at the bottom: "Consideration less than $100."

2. The Illinois transfer tax is assessed at the rate of 50 cents for each $500 or fractional part of $500. Proceeds are shared equally by the county and state.

3. The tax is paid by the seller and is based upon the sale price of the property.

4. Where a new mortgage is being secured by the purchaser and the proceeds are to be used by the purchaser in buying the property, the seller will pay a tax on the full sale price. (In this case the property is not being conveyed "subject to" an existing mortgage and thus the amount of this mortgage is not deducted from the sale price.)

5. Where the seller takes back a purchase money mortgage from the purchaser as part of the purchase price, the seller is required to pay a tax on the full sale price. (As in the preceding rule, the property is not being sold "subject to" an existing mortgage; the mortgage note given to the seller is considered by the tax authorities as part of the total consideration.)

6. Where the purchaser takes the property "subject to" an existing mortgage, that mortgage amount is subtracted from the sale price.

Other Transaction Taxes

A number of municipalities have instituted their own transaction taxes in addition to those of the state and county. Local municipal regulations should be examined to determine if an amount is owed, and by whom.

Illinois Department of Revenue

Property Tax Administration Bureau
REAL ESTATE TRANSFER DECLARATION

THE FOLLOWING INFORMATION IS REQUIRED BY THE **REAL ESTATE TRANSFER TAX ACT** (CHAP. 120, PAR. 1003, IL REV. STAT.). PAGES 1 THROUGH 3 ARE TO BE FILLED OUT BY THE SELLERS AND BUYERS OR THEIR AGENTS. ANY WILLFUL FALSIFICATION OR WILLFUL OMISSION OF INFORMATION IS A CLASS B MISDEMEANOR (CHAP. 120, PAR. 1005, IL REV. STAT.).

EXCEPT AS TO EXEMPT TRANSACTIONS, THE COUNTY RECORDER OF DEEDS IS PROHIBITED BY LAW FROM ACCEPTING ANY DEED FOR RECORDATION UNLESS IT IS ACCOMPANIED BY THIS DECLARATION CONTAINING ALL OF THE INFORMATION REQUESTED HEREIN (CHAP. 120, PAR. 1003, IL REV. STAT.).

For Use By County Recorder's Office
County
Date
Doc. No.
Vol.
Page
Rec'd. By:

PROPERTY IDENTIFICATION

Address of Property _____ Street _____ City or Village _____ Township

Permanent Real Estate Index No. _____   Date of Deed _____ (Month/Year)

Enter Legal Description on Page 2 of this form.   Type of Deed _____

PROPERTY CHARACTERISTICS

Lot Size _____
Acreage _____

Check type of improvement on property
- ☐ Vacant land/lot
- ☐ Residence (Single family or duplex)
- ☐ Mobile home
- ☐ Apartment bldg. (6 units or less)
- ☐ Commercial apartment (Over 6 units)
- ☐ Store, office, commercial bldg.
- ☐ Industrial bldg.
- ☐ Farm, land only
- ☐ Farm, with bldgs.
- ☐ Other (Specify) _____

SALE INFORMATION (The following questions must be answered)

NOTE: If the answer to any of the following questions is "Yes", you do not have to complete the Finance Schedule at the top of pages 2 and 3 of this declaration or the Finance Questions at the bottom of this page.

	Yes	No
1. Is this a transfer between relatives or related corporations?	☐	☐
2. Is this a compulsory transaction in lieu of foreclosure, divorce, court order, condemnation, probate, etc.?	☐	☐
3. Was this a transfer in settlement of an installment contract for deed initiated prior to the current year? Enter contract year _____ .	☐	☐
4. Was the deed any of the following types:	☐	☐

- Court Officer's Deed,
- Quit Claim,
- Trust Deed (Mortgage),
- Conveyance of Less than ¼ Interest,
- Supplemental Deed Given to Correct an Error in Previous Deed.

TERMS OF SALE

Full Actual Consideration (Sale Price) .... $ _____
Less amount of personal property included in purchase .... $ _____
Net consideration for real property .... $ _____
Less value of other real property transferred to seller as part of full consideration .... $ _____
Less amount of mortgage to which the transferred real property remains subject .... $ _____
Net taxable consideration subject to transfer tax .... $ _____

CALCULATION OF TRANSFER TAX

Amount of State of Illinois tax stamps ($.25 per $500 or part thereof of taxable consideration) .... $ _____
Amount of county tax stamps ($ _____ per $500 or part thereof of taxable consideration) .... $ _____
Total Transfer Tax Collected $ _____

Use this space to describe any special circumstances involving this transaction:

FINANCE QUESTIONS: The buyer and seller (or their representatives) must answer the following questions *unless* one or more of the Sale Information questions above was checked "Yes". However, if the Sale Information questions are all marked "No" and any of the following questions are answered "Yes", the buyer or buyer's representative MUST complete the FINANCE SCHEDULE on pages 2 and 3. If the answer to *all* of the questions below is "No", omit completion of the FINANCE SCHEDULE and go directly to the LEGAL DESCRIPTION on page 2 and signature spaces on page 3.

	Yes	No
1. Did the buyer assume the seller's mortgage?	☐	☐
2. Did the seller provide a mortgage in partial or full consideration?	☐	☐
3. Did the seller pay points to secure the buyer's mortgage, including VA and FHA insured loans?	☐	☐
4. Did the seller's mortgagee make interest concessions to the buyer, i.e., offer a "blended" interest rate below market but greater than the seller's existing mortgage rate?	☐	☐
5. Was the financing in any other manner unique or specifically associated with the property being transferred, e.g., builder "buy down" of interest, etc?	☐	☐

12/Transfer of Title

Finance Schedule Instructions:

The Real Estate Transfer Tax Act (Illinois Revised Statutes, Chapter 120, Paragraph 1001-1008) requires information regarding the financing of the purchase price of this property. Willful falsification or omission of this information is a Class B misdemeanor.

Lines A through I of the Finance Schedule must be filled out by the buyer or buyer's representative to account for financing of the purchase. Columns I through VI must be completed for **each** loan involved.

Information required in each column:

I Principal of loan; for an assumed mortgage show principal being assumed.

II Length of time on which monthly payments were calculated. If not applicable mark with an asterisk and explain repayment schedule in Box J on Page 3. **For an assumed mortgage show years remaining from time of sale until loan is fully amortized (paid).**

III If applicable, length of time until mortgage loan must be paid off or renegotiated, or time until balloon payment is due.

IV Nominal interest rate as stated in loan document.

V Indicate if this loan has a FIXED interest rate by entering F in the column, adjustable rate by entering A, or renegotiable by entering R in the column.

VI Show the number of points and dollars paid. Enter points paid by the seller only.

Box J may be used to show more information regarding financing if necessary.

SPECIAL NOTE: If your financing involves other than equal monthly payments you must explain in Box J on Page 3. If your financing involves a "Blend" (i.e. the seller's mortgagee made interest concessions to the buyer), you must explain the specific terms of the financing in Box J on Page 3.

TYPE OF FINANCING: Enter cash downpayment on line A. Enter remainder of purchase price on line B. The total of lines A & B should equal the full consideration indicated on Page 1. If it does not, explain in Box J. **Also, the remainder of purchase price on line B must equal the total principal amounts shown in Column 1 for lines C through I.**

A. Enter Cash Downpayment (include earnest money) - $ _____

B. Enter remainder of Purchase Price - $ _____

C. Purchase Money Mortgage to Seller _____

D. New 1st Mtg. [specify type* _____]

E. New 2nd Mtg. [specify type * _____]

F. New 3rd Mtg. [specify type * _____]

G. Assumption of existing 1st Mtg. _____

H. Assumption of existing 2nd Mtg. _____

I. Other Financing [specify type * _____]

* *Specify type: e.g., Blend, Conventional, Seller Financed, VA/FHA insured, etc.*

LEGAL DESCRIPTION

Section_____ Township_____ Range_____

Enter complete legal description in this area:

FINANCE SCHEDULE

	I	TERM		IV	V	VI	
	Amount of Principal ($'s)	II Amortization Period (Years Remaining)	III Term To Balloon or Renegotiation (Years)	Interest Rate (%)	Type of Interest Rate	Points Paid by Seller To Obtain Financing	
						%	$'s
A.	X X X X X X X	X X X X X X X	X X X X X X X	X X X X X X X	X X X X	X X X X	X X X X X X X
B.	X X X X X X X	X X X X X X X	X X X X X X X	X X X X X X X	X X X X	X X X X	X X X X X X X
C.							
D.							
E.							
F.							
G.							
H.							
I.							

Official Use Only

J. Use this space to explain replies in Finance Schedule if necessary and to explain any characteristics of the financing of this transaction that may have impacted the sale price.

BUYER:
I hereby declare the Finance Schedule on Pages 2 and 3 of this declaration to be true and correct. *(NOTE: Any person who willfully falsifies or omits any information required in this declaration shall be guilty of a Class B Misdemeanor.)*

Buyer or Name of person filling out the Finance Schedule for the buyer: _____ _____
                                                                      Please Print   Signature

Address _____ Telephone _____

BUYER & SELLER:
The buyer and seller hereby declare the full actual consideration and above facts contained in this declaration (excluding the Finance Schedule) to be true and correct. *(NOTE: Any person who willfully falsifies or omits any information required in this declaration shall be guilty of a Class B Misdemeanor.)*

_____
Name and Current Residence of Seller (Please Print)

Signature: _____
           Seller or Agent

_____
Name and Current Residence of Buyer (Please Print)

Signature: _____
           Buyer or Agent

Mail tax bill to: _____ _____ _____
                  Name   Street   City

PREPARER:
Chapter 120, Paragraph 1003, IL Rev. Statutes, requires the following information to be completed:

Name of person filling out the real estate transfer declaration for the buyer and seller: _____
                                                                                          Please Print

Address _____ Telephone _____

THIS BOX FOR USE BY DEPARTMENT OF REVENUE ONLY:

Adjustment NONE ☐
            CHART ☐
            J. ☐

Initial _____ Date _____

12/Transfer of Title 53

ASSESSMENT INFORMATION ON SOLD PROPERTIES

This page is to be completed by the County Assessor or Supervisor of Assessments. The form is to be mailed to Illinois Department of Revenue, 303 East Monroe, P.O. Box 4058, Springfield, IL 62708

1. ENTER BRIEF **LEGAL DESCRIPTION** OF PROPERTY AS IT APPEARS ON ASSESSMENT BOOKS.

   _____
   _____
   _____
   _____

2. INSTRUCTIONS FOR COMPLETING PROPERTY DESCRIPTION CODES:

    (a) Enter Permanent Real Estate Index Number. Enter the property use code in the Unit No. boxes if using the IL Real Property Appraisal Manual, or circle the appropriate letter if using the codes in the IL Property Tax Manual. Enter the assessment Quadrant if applicable.

    (b) County & Township: Use codes from Department Code Sheets.   (d) Date of Deed: Enter month, and year, from Page 1 of declaration.

    (c) Class of Property: For Cook County, see Property Type Code Sheet.   (e) Acreage: For Class 51 and 61 Property, enter number of acres: for Class 71 and 81 Property, leave blank.

    For Downstate Counties: enter

    51 (if 5 acres or more with no building)   71 (if under 5 acres with no building)
    61 (if 5 acres or more with a building)   81 (if under 5 acres with a building)

PERMANENT REAL ESTATE INDEX NO.

(a) ☐☐ ☐☐ ☐☐☐ ☐☐☐ ☐☐☐ / F, FO, FI, C, I, R Circle One ☐ ASSM'T QUAD.
    TWP. SEC. BLOCK PARCEL UNIT

(b) County ☐☐
    Township ☐☐

(c) Class ☐☐

              Month   Year
(d) Date of Deed ☐☐ ☐☐

(e) Acreage (Round to nearest full acre) ☐☐☐

Comments by Supervisor of Assessments or County Assessor:

3. ASSESSED VALUE DATA

    Enter assessed value as finally adjusted by the Board of Review or Appeals for the year prior to the date of sale. Where assessment is partial or split, designate with a large "P" or "S" on the assessment boxes.

    YEAR PRIOR TO SALE 19_____   The following questions must be answered:

Book No.	Page	Line

    Yes No
    1. ☐ ☐ Is this a 20e assessment?
    2. ☐ ☐ Is this a partial assessment? (i.e., improvement not completed on assessment date)
    3. ☐ ☐ Is this a split (division)?
    4. ☐ ☐ Has an improvement been added or removed since January 1 of the year prior to the sale?
    5. ☐ ☐ Does assessment shown reflect all Board of Review or Appeals action for the year indicated (including Board of Review equalization factors)?

    Land ☐☐,☐☐☐,☐☐☐
    Bldgs. ☐☐,☐☐☐,☐☐☐
    Total ☐☐,☐☐☐,☐☐☐

I hereby certify that the information shown relates to the property described in the declaration and that the assessed valuations are for the property included in the transfer.

Dated this _____ day of

_____, 19____.

_____
Supervisor of Assessments or County Assessor

FOR DEPARTMENT USE ONLY

Full Consideration
☐☐,☐☐☐,☐☐☐

☐ ☐ Multiple Parcel Indicator

Adjusted Consideration
☐☐,☐☐☐,☐☐☐

Tab Number: _____

File Maintenance
☐☐☐☐☐

QUESTIONS

1. Mr. Jones, who is survived by a spouse and one child, owned Illinois real estate in fee simple. Since he died intestate:

    a. the county inherits all his real property.
    b. the spouse and the child share the estate equally.
    c. the spouse receives one-third and the child two-thirds.
    d. the spouse receives two-thirds and the child receives one-third.

2. To execute a valid will in Illinois:

    a. the testator must be at least 18 years old and of sound mind.
    b. the will must be in writing and signed by the testator.
    c. the will must be witnessed by two persons who will not benefit by the will.
    d. all of the above

3. An Illinois bargain and sale deed:

    a. warrants that the grantor has fee simple title.
    b. is similar to bargain and sale deeds used in many neighboring states.
    c. conveys to the grantee any future title the grantor may acquire.
    d. all of the above

4. Illinois transfer tax:

    a. is customarily paid by the buyer.
    b. is computed on the sale price less the amount of any existing mortgage to which the property remains subject.
    c. is not required if the actual total consideration is less than $500.
    d. all of the above

5. Which of the following is (are) exempt from the Illinois transfer tax?

    a. a deed conveying a property owned by a charitable institution
    b. a court deed partitioning a joint tenancy
    c. deeds for property valued at less than $100
    d. all of the above

6. Hess, a long-time Illinois resident who owned considerable real and personal property, died testate devising only $10,000 to his wife, Martha, who was his sole survivor. Martha renounced the will. Which of the following is a true statement?

    a. The entire will is invalid.
    b. Martha is entitled to a one-quarter share of all property.
    c. Martha is entitled to one-half of the entire estate.
    d. Since Hess left no descendants, Martha is entitled to the entire estate by the law of descent.

7. Barry Lawngrow bought a home in Mt. Prospect. Which is (are) true?

    a. At closing he will pay transfer taxes to the state and the county.
    b. The county receives $.25 for every $500 of taxable consideration.
    c. His wife Barbara acquires a dower right interest.
    d. all of the above

8. An Illinois resident died intestate leaving a surviving mother and brother. The estate would be:

    a. left entirely to the mother.
    b. divided equally between the two.
    c. divided so that the mother receives two-thirds and the brother receives one-third.
    d. divided so that the mother receives one-third and the brother receives two-thirds.

9. James Raft owned Illinois real estate as a sole owner and died intestate leaving his wife and their one child surviving him. After the decedent's debts and taxes are paid, the child will own:

    a. two-thirds in fee simple.
    b. one-third in fee simple.
    c. all in fee simple.
    d. none of the above

10. Chartel owned a parcel of Illinois real estate and he died intestate, leaving no heirs or kin. His real estate is now owned by:

    a. his deceased father's estate.
    b. the public administrator.
    c. the county in which it is located.
    d. none of the above

11. Claire and Robert Baskin owned their Peoria home in joint tenancy. Because they each had one child by a previous marriage, both of them made wills that provided for one-half of their entire estate to go to the surviving spouse and the remaining half to be divided equally between the two children. After Claire was killed in an automobile accident, each child's share of the family residence was:

    a. one-fourth
    b. one-third.
    c. one-half.
    d. none.

12. Ev Roman has a home with a $40,000 mortgage. If she sells the house to Greta Mall for $80,000:

    a. Ev must pay $80 transfer taxes if she pays off the mortgage with the proceeds of the sale.
    b. Greta must pay Roman $80,080 for the home.
    c. Mall must pay $1.00 for every $1,000 of consideration.
    d. Roman must pay $1.00 for every $1,000 of consideration.

13. A parcel of real estate encumbered with a mortgage is being sold for $10,000. The purchaser agrees to take title subject to this mortgage with a present balance of $4,800 and to pay $5,200 in cash upon receipt of the seller's deed. What amount of stamps must the seller affix to the deed?

    a. $5.50
    b. $5.20
    c. $5.00
    d. $4.80

14. Mira Dyne sells her condominium to Jesse Johnson for $80,000. Which is (are) true?

    I. If she takes back a purchase money mortgage of $60,000, her total tax due to the county and state is $60.
    II. If she lets Johnson take title subject to her $50,000 mortgage, she will pay a $30 total tax to the county and state.

    a. I only   c. both I and II
    b. II only   d. neither I nor II

12/Transfer of Title   57

15. Ms. Smith agreed to sell her home for $27,000. There is an existing mortgage on the property with an unpaid balance of $12,500. This mortgage has a prepayment option and the seller will pay the $12,500 balance with the proceeds she receives from the sale. The purchaser, who has arranged for a mortgage loan of $17,500, will pay the remaining $9,500 in cash. Because of the two loan transactions, it is necessary to close the sale through an escrow. What amount of transfer tax is Ms. Smith required to affix to her deed conveying this property?

    a. $12.50
    b. $14.50
    c. $17.50
    d. $27.00

16. Mr. Morgan has a deed prepared conveying a piece of his real estate to his son as a gift. The deed contains a statement that it was given in "consideration of ten dollars and love and affection." The property had a reasonable market value of $12,000. Mr. Morgan is required to attach what amount of transfer stamps to his executed deed?

    a. $12.00
    b. $10.00
    c. $1.00
    d. none

13

Title Records

RECORDER OF DEEDS

A Recorder of Deeds is elected in each Illinois county with a population of 60,000 or more. In those counties with a population of less than 60,000, the County Clerk serves as the Recorder of Deeds.

Deeds, mortgages, and other instruments relating to real estate must be recorded in the county where the real estate is located in order to give legal or constructive notice to the world of the interest of the parties. When the property is registered under the Land Registration Act (Torrens System), the instruments must be filed with the Registrar of Titles (see below). Most documents are not required by law to be filed or recorded within a specified period of time. However, creditors and subsequent purchasers who have no actual notice of the content of the documents affecting real estate interests are charged with legal or constructive notice of such documents only as of the date on which the documents are recorded. Tax deeds, by law, must be recorded within one year after the redemption period expires. In the event a tax deed is not recorded or filed within this period, the deed becomes null and void.

The state legislature in Illinois has set forth specific requirements in order for a deed to be accepted for recording in Illinois:

1. The name of the grantor must be typed or printed below his or her signature.

2. If the land involved is a tract of fewer than five acres, the provisions of the Illinois Plat Act relative to recording are to be followed. If the conveyance of such a tract is exempt from the Plat Act, an affidavit setting forth the reason for the exemption may be required by the Recorder at the time of recording or filing.

3. A real estate transfer declaration (see pages 51-53) must accompany each conveyance presented for recording. This declaration must indicate the amount of transfer tax, if any, and such taxes must be paid by stamps, which must be attached to the conveyance before or after recording.

4. A deed must include the address of the grantee.

5. A deed in a foreign language, although valid between the parties, does not give constructive notice unless, when recorded, it has attached to it a translation prepared by an official source such as the local consulate office of the country in which the language is used. This requirement in effect means that the contents of a deed or other document must be in English in order that it may give constructive notice when it has been recorded.

REGISTRAR OF TITLES (TORRENS SYSTEM)

The Torrens System of land registration is authorized by the Illinois Land Registration Act of 1897. To become operative an any county of the State of Illinois, the System must be approved by a referendum of the voters of the county. Even after the System has been approved, it does not affect any of the real property within the county unless the owner files a land registration proceeding in the circuit court to register the title to his or her specific parcel of real estate. All land not so registered remains under the County Recorder's office system. <u>Cook County is the only county in Illinois that has approthe Land Registration System.</u> In Cook County the County Recorder also performs the duties of the Registrar of Titles, although these offices need not be held by the same person.

Under the Torrens System, the Registrar retains the original of all documents filed in his office affecting real estate registered under the System. When documents have been executed in duplicate, both the original and duplicate copies may be delivered to the Registrar at the time of recording. The duplicate will be returned to the property owner after registration.

A 1983 amendemnt to the Land Registration Act allows, for the first time in Illinois, removal of real estate parcels from the Torrens System. This amendment does away with the old axiom, "Once in Torrens, always in Torrens." The removal procedure the amendment establishes is quite complex, so the action should be undertaken with the aid of an attorney competent in real estate law.

The Land Registration Act also provides that title to Torrens-registered property can never be acquired through a claim af adverse possession. This gives an owner of registered land protection against such claims.

Any registered owner who sustains any damage or loss by reason of any error in the registration of his or her title may file a claim with the County Board or bring suit against the county. A cash indemnity fund is maintained to cover any such claims.

ACKNOWLEDGMENT

By act of the Illinois legislature, provision is made for individuals executing instruments affecting real property to acknowledge their signatures on such instruments. It is customary for most documents to be acknowledged before a notary public, although other officials designated by the State--court clerks and county clerks--are legally authorized to take acknowledgments. When the acknowledgment is taken before a notary public, the notary's official seal must be affixed to the document.

The statute also sets forth how such instruments may be acknowledged in states other than Illinois and in foreign countries.

Acknowledgments are not necessary to validate a conveyance or to entitle a deed to be recorded although it is customary to do so. However, when acknowledged, the conveyance may be read as evidence in court without further proof of execution. And, as a general practice, deeds, mortgages, releases and similar documents are always acknowledged before delivery.

QUESTIONS

1. In order for a deed to be recorded it must:

    a. have the name of the grantor typed or printed below his or her signature.
    b. include the address of the grantee.
    c. be accompanied by a signed state real estate transfer declaration.
    d. all of the above

2. Land registered under the Torrens System in Illinois:

    a. must be registered in the grantor's name before title to the land can be transferred by his or her deed.
    b. is subject to transfer by means of adverse possession.
    c. may be found in Cook, Lake, and DuPage counties.
    d. all of the above

3. Tax deeds:

    a. must be recorded within one year after expiration of the redemption period.
    b. are the only deeds that must be recorded within a specific period.
    c. provide actual notice to creditors affected by the transfer of title.
    d. a and b above

4. Susan Johnson, a Chicago resident, purchases farm land in southern Illinois as an investment. The deed to her:

    a. should be recorded in Cook County where she lives.
    b. must be recorded within two years of purchase.
    c. should be recorded in the county where the property is located.
    d. provides constructive notice of ownership.

5. Constructive notice of a mortgage lien on a specific piece of real property is given when the mortgage is:

    a. recorded in the county where the owner resides.
    b. acknowledged.
    c. both a and b above
    d. none of the above

6. Notary acknowledgment of the signatures on a deed:

    a. is necessary for a deed to be recorded.
    b. is necessary for a deed to be valid.
    c. is proof in a court of law of execution by the grantor.
    d. all of the above

7. Documents affecting land registered under the Land Registration Act (Torrens System) must always be filed with:

    a. the Recorder of Deeds.
    b. the Registrar of Titles.
    c. The Director of Land Registration.
    d. either a or b above

8. Arnie Able sold a house to Bobby Baker, who immediately occupied it but in his haste neglected to have the deed to him recorded. Able, somewhat absent-minded but of sound mind, later sold the same house to Carl Crumpwell, who had his deed recorded but did not make a prior inspection of the property. A court would probably hold that:

    a. Bobby Baker owned the property.
    b. Carl Crumpwell owned the property.
    c. Arnie Able owned the property.
    d. Baker and Crumpwell owned the property as tenants in common.

9. Stella Starlight owns a condominium townhouse in Glenview that is registered in Torrens. Two and a half years ago she moved to Florida, thinking she'd return summers and live in the townhouse. However, she hasn't returned yet. Her former son-in-law, Sam Snatch, stole the keys from Stella's daughter and has been openly living in the townhouse for over two years. Sam:

    a. may have a successful ownership claim of the townhouse after another five years.
    b. may have a successful ownership claim of the townhouse after another 18 years.
    c. may not successfully make a present or future ownership claim of the townhouse.
    d. either a or b, depending upon the court's decision

10. Joan Muldowney buys a home in the Village of Palatine that is registered in the Cook County Torrens Office. She does not like the delay she encountered in getting her copy of the certificate of title. What can happen?

   I. She may collect damages from the county if the Torrens Office makes mistakes.
   II. The Torrens Registrar, after changing the register to record the new owners, will always make and keep a duplicate copy of the original returned to the owner.

   a. I only
   b. II only
   c. both I and II
   d. neither I nor II

14

Real Estate License Laws

Calf. 1917

On January 1, 1984, the Illinois Real Estate License Act superseded the Real Estate Brokers and Salesmen License Act of 1973, which had superseded the original Real Estate Broker Registration Act of 1921. The intent of the legislature in enacting the current Act was to "evaluate the competency of persons engaged in the real estate business and to regulate such business for the protection of the public."

The Act may be found in the Illinois Revised Statutes, Chapter 111, beginning with paragraph 5801. The discussion below will refer to section numbers of the Act itself, rather than the paragraph numbers of the Statutes.

In addition to administering the provisions of the Act, the Illinois Department of Registration and Education is empowered under Section 9 to "issue rules, consistent with the provisions of this Act, for the administration and enforcement thereof and may prescribe forms which shall be used in connection therewith." As these rules and forms are changed from time to time, the student is advised to obtain current copies from the Department. The rules used under the old Act still apply as of this writing, with revisions expected after September 1984.

ADMINISTRATION OF LICENSE LAWS

As noted, the Department of Registration and Education has the authority to administer the License Act and to make and enforce rules and regulations for conducting license examinations, issuing and renewing licenses, and suspending or revoking licenses. Section 31 gives the Department the authority to regulate, license, and set standards for real estate schools.

Actions of the Director of the Department, however, must be made only after considering the recommendations of the Real Estate Administration and Disciplinary Board. The Act specifically prevents the Department from acting on matters of nonresidential licenses (Section 14), penalties for licensees (Section 18), regulation of real estate schools (Section 31), conduct of hearings on license issuance, renewal, suspension, revocation, censure, reprimand, or imposition of civil penalties (Section 20a), and restoration of suspended or revoked licenses (Section 20j) without the action of the Board, including a written report from them.

The Real Estate Administration and Disciplinary Board (Section 9)

In addition to its advisory functions, the Real Estate Administration and Disciplinary Board conducts hearings on disciplinary actions against licensees accused of violating the Department's rules or regulations. (Details of the hearing process are discussed beginning on page 81).

Composition of the Board. The Board is made up of seven members, all of whom have been residents and citizens of Illinois for at least six years before their appointment date. Five members must have been active brokers or salespeople for at least ten years, and not affiliated with any regulated real estate school. The other two members represent the general public. Members' terms are for four years, with terms staggered so that no more than two terms expire in the same year. A member may be reappointed, but no individual may serve more than a total of ten years. The Commissioner of Real Estate is the ex-officio Board chairperson, but has no vote.

The Commissioner of Real Estate (Section 10)

The Director of the Department appoints a licensed broker to the position of Commissioner of Real Estate, after considering the recommendations of real estate professionals and organizations. The Commissioner's license is placed on inactive status during his or her term.

The Commissioner's duties include: acting as ex-officio chairperson of the Board; being the direct liaison between the Department, the profession, and real estate organizations and associations; preparing and circulating educational material for licensees; investigating the actions of any person or entity connected with the transfer, sale, rental, or lease of real property; appointing committees to assist the Department in carrying out its duties; and supervising the real estate unit of the Department, subject to the administrative approval of the Director, to whom the Commissioner reports.

REAL ESTATE LICENSING

The Act makes it illegal for anyone to act as a broker, associate broker, or salesperson, or to advertise as one, without a real estate license from the Department of Registration and Education. Under Section 4, any person or firm who performs any of the following services for another and for compensation must be licensed:

- Sells, exchanges, purchases, rents, or leases real estate.

- Offers to sell, exchange, purchase, rent, or lease real estate.

- Negotiates, offers, attempts, or agrees to negotiate the sale, exchange, purchase, rental or leasing of real estate.

- Lists, offers, attempts, or agrees to list real estate for sale, lease or exchange.

- Buys, sells, offers to buy or sell, or otherwise deals in options on real estate or improvements thereon.

- Collects, offers, attempts, or agrees to collect rent for the use of real estate.

- Advertises or represents him- or herself as being engaged in the business of buying, selling, exchanging, renting, or leasing real estate.

- Assists or directs in procuring of prospects intended to result in the sale, exchange, lease, or rental of real estate.

- Assists or directs in the negotiation of any transaction intended to result in the sale, exchange, leasing, or rental of real estate.

Exempt Persons (Section 6)

The provisions of the Act do not apply to the following persons:

1. Owners or lessors who sell, lease, or otherwise deal with their own property in the ways described under Section 4. Also the owner's or lessor's regular employees who perform such acts in the course of the management, sale, or other disposition of their employer's property. Such employees, however, may not perform such acts in connection with a real estate business that deals with property not owned by their employers.

2. Attorneys-in-fact acting under duly executed and recorded power of attorney to convey real estate from the owner or lessor, or performing their duties as attorneys.

3. Any person acting as receiver, trustee in bankruptcy, administrator, executor or guardian, or while acting under a court order or under the authority of a will or a trust instrument.

4. A resident apartment manager working for an owner or building manager, employed to lease the property.

5. Any officer or employee of a federal agency conducting official duties.

6. Any officer or employee of the state government or a political subdivision thereof performing his or her official duties.

7. Any multiple listing service wholly owned by a not-for-profit organization or association of real estate brokers.

8. Any not-for-profit real estate referral system.

9. Railroads and other public utilities regulated by the state of Illinois, or their subsidiaries or affiliates, and the employees of such organizations. This exemption applies only to the portions of the organization's business that are regulated.

Regulation of Rental Finding Services

Definition. Rule XVII defines a rental finding service as any business that finds, attempts to find, or offers to find for any person for consideration a unit of rental real estate not owned or leased by such business. Any person, association, copartnership, or corporation that operates a rental finding service must obtain a broker's license and comply with all provisions of the Real Estate License Act. General circulation newspapers that advertise rental property and listing contracts between owners or lessors of real estate and registrants are exempt from this rule.

Contract. Before a finding service accepts a consideration, it must enter into a written contract with the person for whom such services are to be performed and deliver a copy of the contract to the prospective tenant. The contract must include:

1. The term of the contract

2. A statement about the refund or nonrefund of the fee paid in advance. The events on which a refund may be based must occur within 90 days after the date of the contract. Once a refund has been demanded it must be paid within 10 days.

3. A statement, if applicable, that some or all the rental units listed were obtained from previously published newspaper advertisements.

4. The type of rental unit and geographic area desired, and the rent the prospective tenant is willing to pay.

5. The total amount to be paid to the finding service. The amount that has been paid in advance must be clearly stated in the contract.

6. A detailed statement of the services to be performed.

7. A statement that the contract will not be valid if information about rental units is not current or accurate. A listing for a unit that has not been available for rent for over two days is not considered current.

8. A statement that information about rental units may be up to two days old.

9. A statement requiring the service to refund all fees if the contract becomes invalid.

Disclosure. A finding service must provide prospective tenants with the following information:

1. The name, address, and telephone number of the owner of each rental unit or his or her authorized agent.

2. A description of the unit.

3. The amount of rent requested.

4. The amount of security deposit required.

5. A statement describing utilities included in the rent.

6. Occupancy date and term of the lease.

7. A statement setting forth the source of the rental information (owner, agent, newspaper, and so forth).

8. Any other information of concern to the prospective tenant.

<u>Permission of owner</u>. A rental finding service may not list any rental unit without the permission of the unit's owner.

<u>Advertising</u>. If a finding service advertises in newspapers, magazines, or other media any rental unit that was originally advertised in a newspaper, it must include the following statement in every advertisement:

> Some or all of the rental units appearing in this advertisement were obtained from previous newspaper advertisements.

<u>Violation</u>. A licensee who violates any provision of this rule, including failure to refund a finding fee to anyone entitled to a refund, will be said to have demonstrated unworthiness or incompetence as a broker and may have his or her license revoked.

Real Estate Defined (Section 4)

Under the Act, real estate includes real property in the state or elsewhere, so an <u>Illinois resident</u> selling property in another state is still required to hold an Illinois real estate license.

LICENSE CATEGORIES AND REQUIREMENTS

The Act designates three categories of real estate licensees: brokers, associate brokers, and salespeople. The law provides general requirements for all license applicants, as well as requirements and limitations specific to each kind of license.

General Requirements (Section 11)

All license applicants must pass the written examination authorized by the Department. Applications for the exam must contain evidence that the applicant is at least 21 years old and that the applicant has completed a four-year high school course or an equivalent approved by the Illinois State Board of Education.

Broker (Section 4)

A broker is defined as anyone who performs any of the services listed on page 66 and 67 for another for compensation, but is not a salesperson, partnership, or corporation.

<u>Requirements</u>. Applicants for the broker's license must have served as active salespeople for at least one of the three years immediately prior to

application, and either have completed at least 90 classroom hours in real estate courses or correspondence courses approved by the Board, or have received a baccalaureate degree including at least minor courses in real estate or related material from a Board-approved college or university.

These requirements do not apply to anyone who has been admitted to practice law by the Supreme Court of Illinois.

Associate Broker (Section 4)

An associate broker may perform the activities permitted to a broker, but is employed or associated as an independent contractor with another broker, and may not employ salespeople. The associate broker status is noted on the license. To obtain a full broker's license, the associate broker must apply to the Department and pay the required fee. When the broker's license is received, the associate broker must terminate his or her association with the sponsoring broker.

Requirements. Requirements for an associate broker's license are the same as for a broker's license.

Salesperson (Section 11)

A salesperson is anyone who engages in the activities permitted to a broker, but is employed by a broker or associated with one by a written contract, and is not a broker or associate broker.

Requirements. Except for applicants who have been admitted to practice law by the Illinois Supreme Court, those seeking a salesperson's license must show that they have completed at least 30 classroom hours of an approved real estate course, or an equivalent correspondence course approved by the Board. Applicants must be at least 21 years old, but those 18 through 20 may apply if they can show that they have completed at least two years of study past the high school level, with major emphasis on real estate courses, in a school approved by the Department.

Inactive Status (Section 13)

A licensee may receive a license as an inactive broker, associate broker, or salesperson by applying to the Department, as long as he or she continues to reside in Illinois. The advantage to this step is that the licensee need not pay annual renewal fees while not working in the real estate field. Simply allowing a license to lapse requires payment of all back annual fees before it will be renewed. While on inactive status, the licensee may not engage in the real estate business, nor accept commissions or finders' fees.

Anyone who remains on inactive status (or allows his or her license to lapse) for more than five but less than seven years is not allowed to reregister for active status until completing at least 15 hours of real estate refresher courses at an approved school. Any license not renewed by the end of seven years from the last expiration date can no longer be reinstated.

A return to active status within the allowable time limits is accomplished by sending an application to the Department, accompanied by the proper fee.

Corporations and Partnerships (Section 3)

Corporations and partnerships may receive broker's licenses under the following conditions:

> Every partner or corporate officer who actively participates in the organization's brokerage business holds a broker's license.

> Every employee who acts as a salesperson for the organization holds a salesperson's license.

Under General Rule III, every corporation, partnership, or association must report to the Department the name and address of each officer, director, partner, or person holding at least a 10 percent interest in the company. Deadline is February 28 of each year.

The same rule withholds licensing from any association, corporation, or partnership if any individual salesperson or group of salespeople owns more than 49 percent of the shares of stocks or ownership interest in the firm. This provision does not prohibit a salesperson from owning stock in a company, but rather is designed to prevent persons who do not hold brokers' certificates from dictating company policy or exerting other controls usually exercised by the corporate officers of brokerage firms.

The Written Examination (Section 12)

Anyone applying for an original broker's, associate broker's, or salesperson's license must take a written exam given under the supervision of the Board or by an approved independent testing service. The questions are to provide the Department with a way to determine "the trustworthiness of the applicant, and the applicant's competency to transact the business of broker or salesperson...in such a manner as to safeguard the interests of the public." At present the exams are administered by the Educational Testing Service (ETS). The Appendix that concludes this book describes the test and offers samples of the kinds of questions applicants are likely to encounter.

To be scheduled for a licensing examination, the applicant must submit to ETS:

1. a completed and signed application form;
2. the required testing fee; and
3. proof that he or she has fulfilled the state real estate education requirement in the form of a school transcript with the embossed school seal and the original signature of any authorized school official. (This proof may be brought in on the examination date if an additional fee is paid for that privilege.)

At present, the examinations are given monthly at locations throughout the state. Exact dates and locations for testing may be obtained from ETS. Each applicant must request a specific date and location for the exam. Applications must be postmarked no later than the filing deadline (approximately one month before the exam date). If a testing center is filled, applicants will be reassigned to the nearest open center. To change a test location or date, the applicant must notify ETS.

After verifying the application, ETS will forward an admission ticket showing the test date and location. This ticket must be presented at the test center along with additional identification that shows a photo and a signature of the applicant.

ETS will notify applicants of the test results within two or three weeks. Persons who fail the test may retake it indefinitely provided that they meet all the requirements for examination and submit an examination fee with each application for testing. ETS has centers in Illinois where those who failed either exam can retake it without preregistering, upon payment of an additional fee.

The License Application

Those who pass the written examination will receive an application form for licensure from ETS. This application must be completed and filed with the Department of Registration and Education within one year of completing the examination. Failure to do so will result in the applicant having to retake the examination.

The license applications for either the broker's or the salesperson's license must be accompanied by checks to cover a processing fee, Recovery Fund fee, and the Research and Education Fund fee. Those failing to qualify for the license may have the fees for the Recovery Fund and the Research and Education Fund refunded.

THE REAL ESTATE LICENSE (Section 13)

Applicants who have met all the requirements will receive a license from the Department. The license will specify whether the individual is authorized to act as a broker, associate broker, or salesperson. This license is to be displayed conspicuously in the holder's place of business. In addition to the license, the Department will issue a pocket card to each licensee. This card authorizes the bearer to engage in the activity named (broker, associate broker, or salesperson) for the current year. Licensees must carry this card when engaging in a licensed activity. Associate brokers and salespeople must also carry a sponsor card.

Sponsor Cards (Section 13)

The Department provides forms upon which brokers are required to prepare sponsor cards for salespeople and associate brokers employed by or associated with them. Recipients of sponsor cards must carry them, along with their pocket cards, and display them on demand when engaging in licensable activities. It is illegal for a salesperson or associate broker to engage in the real estate business without a valid sponsor card as well as a current license and pocket card.

When a broker prepares a sponsor card, he or she is required to send a duplicate to the Department within 24 hours of issuance. This card remains at all times the property of the broker.

Salespeople and associate brokers who terminate their employment or association with a sponsoring broker must return their sponsor cards to that broker within 24 hours of termination. Return is to be made in person or by registered or certified mail, return receipt requested. It is a violation of the Act for a salesperson or associate broker to accept employment or association with a new broker without returning the old sponsor card.

A similar requirement applies when a broker changes his or her place of business. Salespeople and associate brokers must immediately be issued new sponsor cards, and the Department notified of the change. Again, duplicates of the new sponsor cards must be sent to the Department within 24 hours.

When a broker's license is expired, terminated, revoked, or suspended, each sponsor card that the broker has issued is also suspended until his or her license is reinstated. Affected associate brokers and salespeople may still terminate their connection to the suspended broker, and resume their real estate activities when they are issued a sponsor card by a new broker.

When a salesperson or associate broker has terminated his or her connection with a broker, the broker must give the Department that person's sponsor card within two days, or notify the Department in writing of the termination and the reason the sponsor card has not been sent.

Commissions

As stated in Chapter 5, a commission for performance of real estate activities is always paid to the principal broker, who then pays compensation to the salesperson. No person, partnership, or corporation may bring court action in Illinois to collect compensaion for the performance of any real estate activity unless such person is a licensed real estate broker and the license was in effect before the agreement for compensation was negotiated or an offer of services was made. For example, a neighbor who helps you sell your home may not sue you for a commission payment unless he or she is a registered broker with whom you have a listing agreement. Furthermore, it is unlawful for a licensed salesperson to accept a commission or valuable consideration from anyone except his or her employer.

Nonresident Licenses (Section 14)

Brokers who live in states bordering Illinois which have reciprocal licensing agreements with Illinois may be issued nonresident broker's licenses, if the following conditions are met:

1. the broker holds a broker's license in his or her home state;

2. the licensing standards of that state are substantially equivalent to those of Illinois;

3. the broker has been active in the home state for at least the two years prior to the application;

4. the broker maintains a definite place of business in the home state; and

5. the broker furnished the department with a sealed statement from his or her home state licensing authority to the effect that the broker has an active license, is in good standing, and has no pending complaints against him or her.

Nonresident salespeople who are employed by or associated with a nonresident broker may receive nonresident licenses at the discretion of the Department. Their sponsoring brokers must issue them sponsor cards and comply with all other rules and regulations of the Department.

Those applying for nonresident licenses must furnish the Department with certified copies of their home-state licenses. They must also pay the same license fees that are required of resident brokers and salespeople. Prospective nonresident licensees must also agree in writing to abide by all provisions of the Act and to submit to the Department's jurisdiction.

Applicants for nonresident licenses must, in addition, file with the Department a written consent appointing the Director to act as his or her agent upon whom all judicial and other process or legal notices directed to the licensee may be served. The applicant further agrees that such service is binding, and that the Director's authority in this regard remains in effect as long as the licensee has any liability outstanding in Illinois. The written agreement specifies that any such legal process served on the Director as agent has the same legal validity as if it were served directly on the licensee.

Renewal

License holders may renew their licenses by paying the required fee during the month before the license expires. Licenses expired for less than seven years may be renewed by paying all lapsed renewal fees, plus, for a broker or associate broker, a $39 fee; or for a salesperson, a fee of $29. However, if the license has been expired for more than five years, the holder must first take a 15-hour real estate refresher course approved by the Department. A license that has lapsed for seven years or more cannot be renewed.

Exceptions. Licensees engaged in the following activities at the time of license expiration may reinstate without paying lapsed renewal fees or reinstatement fees if they inform the Department of the activity within two years after it ends:

1. federal active military service;

2. military training; or

3. serving as Commissioner of Real Estate.

License Fees (Section 15)

Applicants for real estate licenses are subject to certain fees in addition to the testing fee paid to ETS when applying for an examination. The following payments must be submitted to the Department with the license application:

	Broker/ Associate Broker	Salesperson
Processing fee	$50	$25
Recovery Fund fee	10	10
Real Estate Research and Education Fund fee	4	4
Total	$64	$39

A broker's license for a partnership, association, or corporation is $54.

License Renewal

The following fees are charged for license renewal:

broker or associate broker, $10/year (renewed biennially)

salesperson, $5/year (renewed biennially)

partnership or corporation, $20/year (renewed biennially)

real estate school, $300/year

real estate school branch, $100 per branch/year

real estate instructor, $10/year

License terms are set by rule. Currently, brokers and associate brokers must renew every other year in January. Salespeople renew every other year in March. The student should check with the Department for the latest information on license renewal periods.

Other Fees

Reinstatement of lapsed salesperson's license (includes $4 for Real Estate Research and Education Fund [REREF] and $10 for the Real Estate Recovery Fund), plus all lapsed renewal fees, $29

Reinstatement of lapsed broker's license (includes $4 to REREF and $10 to Recovery Fund), plus all lapsed renewal fees, $39

Reinstatement of salesperson's license after a period on inactive status (includes $4 for REREF and $10 for the Recovery Fund), $34

Reinstatement of a broker's or associate broker's license after inactive status (including REREF and Recovery Fund fees as above), $44

License as inactive salesperson, $10

License as inactive broker or associate broker, $15

Branch office license, $10

Branch office renewal, $10

Branch office transfer, $10 per branch

Duplicate license or pocket card, $10

Certification of licensee's record, $10

Recording duplicate sponsor card, $10

PLACE OF BUSINESS

Following is a summary of the Department's Rule II requirements for real estate offices and branch offices.

The broker's office or place of business cannot be located in any retail sales establishment unless it is separated from the main retail business as a separate and distinct area within that establishment. The Department must be notified immediately in writing of any change of principal or branch business location.

Only a real estate broker or associate broker may supervise or have control of a real estate office or branch office. However, a broker or associate broker shall be in direct operational control of only one office or branch and then only if the broker's principal occupation is real estate. The employing broker must execute a contract stating his or her duties with each associate broker who supervises a branch office.

Requirements for branch offices. To open a branch office, a broker must apply to the Department for a special license bearing the broker's name and license number as well as the address of the branch office and the name and license number of the broker or associate broker in charge of the office. These certificates must also be conspicuously displayed at those locations.

When application is made for a branch office license or renewal, the broker must inform the Department of the name and certificate number of the active broker or associate broker who is to manage the office. The name of the broker or associate broker managing the branch office must appear on the branch office certificate because, when such a manager terminates his or her employment, the branch office must cease operation until a new manager is employed and a new branch office license issued. Nothing in this rule relieves the principal broker of the legal responsibility for the overall supervision of all branch offices.

REFUSAL, SUSPENSION, OR REVOCATION OF LICENSE, OR CIVIL PENALTIES (Section 18)

The Department may refuse to issue or renew any license, may suspend or revoke any license, or may censure, reprimand, or impose a civil penalty of not more than $10,000 for any one or a combination of specific reasons. These are

14/Real Estate License Laws   77

listed in Section 18 of the Act. Following is a summary of Section 18 provisions. The above penalties may be invoked when:

- an individual has made false representation in attempting to get a license;

- the licensee has been convicted of a felony or of a crime "an essential element of which is dishonesty or fraud or larceny, embezzlement, obtaining money, property or credit by false pretenses or by means of a confidence game...."

- the licensee has been adjudged insane or mentally incompetent;

- the licensee operates a real estate business in a retail establishment without separating his or her desk, office, or space into an area distinct from the retail business;

- the licensee in performing or attempting to perform or pretending to perform any act as a broker or salesperson, or in handling his or her own property, is found guilty of:

  1. making any substantial misrepresentation, or untruthful advertising (see also Advertising Regulations, p.80);

  2. making any false promises of a character likely to influence, persuade, or induce;

  3. pursuing a continued and flagrant course of misrepresentation or the making of false promises through agents, salespersons, advertising or otherwise:

  4. any misleading or untruthful advertising, or using any trade name or insignia of membership in any real estate organization of which the licensee is not a member;

  5. acting for more than one party in a transaction without the written acknowledgment of all parties for whom the licensee acts;

  6. representing or attempting to represent a broker other than the employer;

  7. failure to account for or to remit for any moneys or documents coming into their possession which belong to others;

  8. failure to maintain and deposit in a special account, separate and apart from a personal or other business account, all moneys belonging to others entrusted to the licensee while acting as a broker, or as escrow agent, or as the temporary custodian of the funds of others until the transaction involved is consummated or terminated; such account shall be noninterest-bearing unless the character of the deposit is such that interest thereon is otherwise required by law, or unless written agreement of the principals to the transaction requires that the deposit be placed in an interest-bearing account;

9. failing to furnish copies upon request of all documents relating to a real estate transaction to all parties executing them;

10. paying a commission or valuable consideration to any person for acts or services performed in violation of this Act;

11. having demonstrated unworthiness or incompetency to act as a broker, associate broker or salesperson in such manner as to endanger the interest of the public;

12. commingling the money or property of others with his or her own;

13. employing any person as a salesperson or associate broker on a purely temporary or single-deal basis as a means of evading the law regarding payment of commission to nonlicensees on some contemplated transactions;

14. permitting the use of his or her license as a broker to enable a salesperson to operate a real estate business without actual participation therein and control thereof by the broker;

15. any other conduct, whether of the same or a different character from that specified in Section 18 of the Act, which constitutes dishonest dealing;

16. displaying a For Rent or For Sale sign on any property without the written consent of an owner or his duly authorized agent, or advertising that any property is for sale or for rent in a newspaper or other publication without the consent of the owner or his or her authorized agent;

17. failing to provide information requested by the Department within 30 days of the request, either as the result of a formal or informal complaint to the Department or as a result of a random audit conducted by the Department, which would indicate a violation of this Act;

18. disregarding or violating any provision of this Act, or the published rules or regulations promulgated by the Department to enforce this Act;

19. advertising any property for sale or advertising any transaction of any kind or character relating to the sale of property by whatsoever means, without clearly disclosing in such advertising one of the following: the name of the firm with which the licensee is associated, if a sole broker evidence of the broker's occupation, or a name with respect to which the broker has complied with the requirements of "An Act in relation to the use of an assumed name in the conduct or transaction of business in this State," approved July 17, 1941, as amended, whether such advertising is done by the broker or by any salesperson or associate broker employed by the broker;

20. using prizes, money, free gifts, or other valuable consideration as inducements to secure: (1) customers to purchase, rent or lease property when the awarding of such prizes, money, free

14/Real Estate License Laws   79

gifts, or other valuable consideration is conditioned upon such purchase, rental or lease; or (2) clients to list properties with licensee. [This does not apply to guaranteed sales plans (see next section).

NOTE: In November 1983, the Illinois Circuit Court issued a declaratory judgment ruling Subsection 20 (reprinted above) unconstitutional. Therefore the prohibition against using prizes, etc., as inducements became unenforceable pending further rulings. The case, <u>Coldwell Banker Residential Real Estate Services of Illinois, Inc. v. Clayton & The Illinois Department of Registration and Education</u> (1983), was appealed to the Illinois Supreme Court, where a ruling was expected by the end of November 1984.

21. influencing or attempting to influence by any words or acts a prospective seller, purchaser, occupant, landlord or tenant of real estate, in connection with viewing, buying or leasing of real estate, so as to promote, or tend to promote, the continuance of maintenance or racially and religiously segregated housing, or so as to retard, obstruct or discourage racially integrated housing on or in any street, block, neighborhood or community;

22. engaging in any act which constitutes a violation of Section 3-102, 3-103, 3-104, or 3-105 of the Illinois Human Rights Act, whether or not a complaint has been filed with or adjudicated by the Human Rights Commission;

23. inducing any party to a contract of sale to break such contract for the purpose of substituting, in lieu thereof, a new contract with a third party;

24. negotiating a sale, exchange or lease of real property directly with an owner or lessor without authority from the listing broker if the licensee knows that the owner or lessor has a written exclusive listing agreement covering the property with another broker;

25. where a licensee, who is also a lawyer, acts as the lawyer for either the buyer or the seller in the same transaction in which such licensee is acting or has acted as a broker or salesperson.

<u>Exception for Guaranteed Sales Plans.</u> Item 20 in the preceding list, which prohibited free gifts and other inducements, specifically does not apply to guaranteed sales plans as defined in the Act. In a guaranteed sales plan, the broker promises to buy a property he or she has listed in the event the property has not been sold within a specified time period.

The Act sets rules for such plans as follows:

- the broker must provide the details of the plan in writing to the party to whom the plan is offered;

- the broker must provide evidence of his or her capacity to abide by the financial commitments undertaken in the plan;

80 ILLINOIS SUPPLEMENT for Modern Real Estate Practice

- the broker must market the listing in the same manner he or she would market any other property, unless the agreement with the seller provides otherwise; and

- a broker who fails to perform on a guaranteed sales plan in strict accordance with its terms is subject to all the penalties provided for violations of the Act, plus a civil penalty of up to $10,000, payable to the injured party.

Advertising Regulations

In addition to the provisions found specifically in the Act, the Department enforces a number of rules and regulations regarding real estate advertising. A summary of these follows.

General Rule IX establishes advertising guidelines for the registrant. Under this rule a broker must include his or her business name in all real estate advertising and promotional material, including newspaper classified ads and promotional stuffers for billing as well as a business card and letterhead. Blind ads using only a box number, street address, or telephone number are prohibited. These restrictions apply to personal real estate advertised by registrants as well as business transactions. A broker may use an assumed name in an advertisement if he or she has properly registered it as required by the Illinois Assumed Name Statute and has advised the Department as required by Rule XIV.

Truth in advertising. Use of "misleading" advertising will not be condoned and can be reason for loss of license. It is considered misleading or untruthful if, when taken as a whole, there is a distinct and reasonable possibility that it will be misunderstood or will deceive the ordinary purchaser, seller, renter, or owner.

Financing. Regulation Z provides strict regulation of real estate advertisements that include mortgage financing terms. General phrases like "liberal terms available" may be used, but if details are given, they must comply with this Act. By the provisions of the Act, the annual percentage rate--which includes all charges--rather than the interest rate alone must be stated. The total finance charge must be specified as well.

Specific credit terms, such as the down payment, monthly payment, dollar amount of the finance charge, or term of the loan, may not be advertised unless the following information is set forth as well: cash price; required down payment; number, amount, and due dates of all payments; and annual percentage rate. The total of all payments to be made over the term of the mortgage must also be specified unless the advertised credit refers to a first mortgage or trust deed to finance acquisition of a dwelling.

Salesperson advertising. A salesperson or associate broker is prohibited from placing an advertisement under his or her own name. All advertising placed by a salesperson must contain the name of and be done under the supervision of his or her employing broker. A salesperson is not even permitted to list his or her name under the heading of Real Estate in the telephone directory without also listing the employing broker.

Advertising signs. Under Illinois law a real estate broker cannot place an advertising sign on any property without the written consent of the owner or authorized agent. Advertising signs are generally defined to mean any advertising display, flags, or bunting including words such as For Sale, Open House, New House, Visitors Welcome, and Home Inspection.

Procedure for Disciplinary Hearings (Section 20)

Complaints may be filed by the Department, the Real Estate Administration and Disciplinary Board, or in the form of a written, verified complaint by any person. The Board then sets up a time and place for a hearing where the accused and the complainant may present evidence and arguments. If the accused fails to appear at the hearing after receiving notice, his or her license may be revoked, or other penalties imposed.

The Department and Board have the power to subpoena witnesses and evidence relating to the complaint, and to administer oaths. At the conclusion of the hearing, the Board will present a written report of its findings and recommendation to the Director. Within 20 days after receiving a copy of the report, the accused may request a rehearing.

If the Director is not satisfied that substantial justice has been done, he or she may order a rehearing by the Board or by a specially appointed committee. The Director is required to give the Board and the Secretary of State a written statement detailing his reasons for disagreeing with their findings, within 30 days before taking a contrary action. If such a statement is not provided within 30 days after the Board's recommendation, the Director has the right to take the action recommended by the Board.

At any time after the suspension or revocation of a license, the Department may reinstate it without examination upon the written recommendation of the Board.

Under the Administrative Review Law, the accused may request a judicial review by petitioning the circuit court of the county of his or her residence. The circuit court's decision, in turn, may be appealed directly to the Illinois Supreme Court.

Criminal Prosecution and Penalties (Section 22)

In addition to the administrative penalties and procedures described above, the License Act provides for criminal prosecution for violations of the Act, to be prosecuted by the State's Attorney of the county where the offense was committed. The Act excludes violations of paragraph 4, subsection e of Section 18 (item 4, p. 77) covering misleading and untruthful advertising and improper use of trade names or insignia, from the criminal prosecution specified for other offenses.

A broker or salesperson convicted by a court of violating the other provisions of the Act is guilty of a class A or C misdemeanor or a class 4 felony. The Act also specifically applies the criminal penalties to those "failing to account for or to remit for any moneys coming into [their] possession which belong to others or commingling the money or other property of [their] principal with [their] own...."

Corporations and partnerships can be convicted of a business offense, and officers and agents who personally participate in or are shown to be accessory to the violation can be prosecuted as individuals, as well, and subject to the prescribed criminal penalties.

Violations of Section 3 of the Act, namely, engaging in real estate business activities without a license, are singled out for harsher penalties than those inflicted for other offenses. The penalties provided by the Act may be summarized as follows:

MISDEMEANORS AND FELONIES BY INDIVIDUALS

	Fines of:	and/or Imprisonment for:
Violation of Section 3, first offense: Class A misdemeanor	not over $1,000	up to one year
Violation of Section 3, second offense: Class 4 felony	not over $10,000	one to 3 years
Violation of other sections, first offense: Class C misdemeanor	not over $500	not over 30 days
Violation of other sections, second offense: Class A misdemeanor	not over $1,000	up to one year

BUSINESS OFFENSES BY CORPORATIONS OR PARTNERSHIPS

	Fines of:	
Violation of Section 3, first offense:	not over $10,000	------------
Violation of Section 3, second offense:	$10,000 - $25,000	------------
Violation of other sections, first offense:	not over $2,000	------------
Violation of other sections, second offense:	$2,000 - $5,000	------------

In addition to criminal prosecution, the Department has the authority to originate an injunction to prevent or stop violations of the Act or to prevent an unlicensed person from acting as a broker or salesperson.

Section 32 of the Act authorizes the use of an injunction to prevent or stop violations of this Act by declaring that violations are "harmful to the public welfare" and a "public nuisance." Court action to enjoin any person from such unlawful activity may be maintained in the name of the people of the state of Illinois by the Attorney General, State's Attorney of the county, the Department, or any resident citizen.

All fines and penalties for violations of the Act are deposited in the Real Estate Recovery Fund in the State Treasury.

THE REAL ESTATE RECOVERY FUND (Section 32)

The Real Estate Recovery Fund was established to provide a means of compensation for losses resulting from acts of registered real estate brokers or salespeople which are in violation of this Act, or which constitute embezzlement, obtaining money by false pretenses, forgery or any other fraud, misrepresentation, discrimination, or deceit on the part of registered brokers or salespersons or of the unlicensed employee of any such broker.

The maximum recovery by any one person from any one act is limited to $10,000 in actual damages together with costs and attorney's fees not to exceed 15 percent of the damages. Losses are limited to actual cash money, as opposed to losses in market value. The maximum liability that will be paid for the acts of a single licensee performed since January 1, 1974, is $50,000. The maximum liability from any one act shall be $50,000 and spread equitably among all aggrieved persons.

Financing

All applicants for original broker's or salesperson's licenses must pay $10 to the Fund at the time of application.

If, on December 31 of any year, the balance in the Fund is less than $1,250,000, every licensee must pay an additional fee of $10 to replenish the fund, payable at the time their certificates are renewed.

Disciplinary Action against the Registrant (Sections 25 and 28)

When the Department pays from the Recovery Fund to settle a claim or satisfy a judgment against a licensed broker or salesperson or an unlicensed employee of a broker, the license of the boker or salesperson is automatically terminated. Such a broker or salesperson is ineligible to receive a new license until he or she has repaid the amount paid out from the Recovery Fund in full plus 8 percent interest. A discharge in bankruptcy does not relieve a person from the penalties and disabilities provided in the Act.

The Department is subrogated to all rights of the judgment creditor and any amounts it may recover shall be deposited in the Fund.

Management of the Fund (Section 26)

The Recovery Fund shall be deposited in the State Treasury and held in a special fund. Funds may be invested and reinvested in the same manner as funds of the State Employee's Retirement System. The interest from the investments shall be deposited in a special fund of the State Treasury known as the Real Estate Research and Education Fund where they may be used only for operation of the Office of Real Estate Research at the University of Illinois.

Recovery from the Fund (Section 25)

No suit for recovery from the Fund shall be started later than two years after the date the alleged violation occurred. Any aggrieved person commencing a suit that may result in collection from the Fund shall notify the Department in writing. The Department may intervene and defend against such a suit.

Before seeking recovery from the Fund, an aggrieved person must first seek and obtain a valid judgment against the offending broker, salesperson, or unlicensed employee on the grounds of fraud, misrepresentation, or deceit. If, after the termination of all proceedings, reviews and appeals, the judgment has not been satisfied in full, the aggrieved may seek a court order directing payment from the Fund. However, the aggrieved individual is required to give 30 days' notice in writing to the Department and the person against whom the judgment is entered, and to prove to the court that he or she has searched for assets of the judgment debtor that could be available to satisfy the judgment. Generally such person must satisfy the court that "he has diligently pursued all remedies against the judgment debtors" before applying to the Fund. The aggrieved party must also prove that the amount of attorney's fees claimed is accurate and reasonable.

OTHER FUNDS

Real Estate Research and Education Fund (Section 16)

A special fund known as the Real Estate Research and Education Fund is kept by the State Treasury for operation of the Office of Real Estate Research at the University of Illinois. Applicants for new licenses and those reinstating inactive or expired licenses must pay $4 toward this fund at the time of making application. Interest earned by investing this fund and the Recovery Fund is the other source of operating income.

Real Estate License Administration Fund (Section 17)

All fees received by the Department under the Act, other than those deposited in the Real Estate Recovery Fund, the Real Estate Research and Education Fund, or in the Department of Central Management Services Printing Revolving Fund, are to be deposited in a special fund in the State Treasury called the Real Estate License Administration Fund. Money from this fund is used for operation of the Department and the Board.

Investigatory Personnel. Section 17 specifies that the Director is to hire one full-time Chief of Real Estate Investigations. In addition, he or she is to hire one full-time investigator and one full-time auditor for every 15,000 licensees.

QUESTIONS

1. In Illinois, a salesperson is not permitted to:

    a. accept a commission from anyone other than his or her employing broker.
    b. own more than 10 percent interest in a brokerage business.
    c. submit an application for the broker's examination without first notifying his or her broker of the intent to do so.
    d. prepare closing statements under any circumstances.

2. In order for a corporation, copartnership, or association to receive a broker's license in Illinois:

    a. every officer or member actively engaged in the real estate business must hold a broker's certificate.
    b. no more than 49 percent of the shares of the company may be held by salespeople.
    c. the business must submit a $54 license processing fee.
    d. all of the above

3. Which of the following meets one of the requirements for a broker's license?

    a. completion of 50 hours in real estate courses
    b. age of at least 21
    c. has been a salesperson for at least six months
    d. has been admitted to the American Bar Association

4. The Department of Registration and Education has revoked broker Ted Beeston's license for commingling earnest money with his own funds. Which of the following is a correct statement?

    a. Beeston may appeal his conviction to the Illinois Circuit Court.
    b. Beeston may have his license reinstated by signing an irrevocable consent form.
    c. Beeston may continue his business for 90 days provided he posts a bond with the Recovery Fund.
    d. Beeston's employees may continue in business for 90 days, since they were not found guilty of any offense.

5. If an aggrieved person is awarded a judgment against a real estate licensee for violations of the Illinois licensing act:

    a. the aggrieved party may immediately apply to the Department for payment from the Recovery Fund for any amount up to $10,000.
    b. the aggrieved party must seek satisfaction of the judgment from the licensee before applying to the court for an order on the Fund.
    c. the aggrieved party has the right to seek satisfaction from the licensee even after being compensated from the Recovery Fund.
    d. all of the above

6. Broker Gayle P. is found to have deposited her buyer's earnest money in her personal money market fund, without telling the buyer. She is subject to the following penalty or penalties, assuming she has never before been convicted of a real estate law violation:

   I. imprisonment of up to one year.
   II. revocation of her license.

   a. I only
   b. II only
   c. both I and II
   d. neither I nor II

7. Allan's broker's license expired three years ago, but he placed ads in the newspaper seeking listings, and continued to act as a broker. He was convicted of acting as a broker without a license two years ago. If found guilty again, he will be penalized for:

   I. a business offense.
   II. a felony.

   a. I only
   b. II only
   c. both I and II
   d. neither I nor II

8. Salesperson Sheila is employed by broker Larry, who failed to renew his broker's license. Sheila:

   a. may continue to take listings for Larry as long as her license remains valid.
   b. may transfer her sponsor card to another broker.
   c. must terminate her employment with Larry and get a sponsor card from a new broker before she can continue to work.
   d. must give her current pocket card to Larry, and get another one from a different broker.

9. In order to sit for the salesperson's examination, an applicant must:

   a. submit an examination application to ETS signed by a prospective employer.
   b. submit an examination fee of $10.25 to the Department.
   c. have successfully completed at least 30 hours of real estate courses.
   d. all of the above

10. Upon successfully passing the licensing examination, an applicant may receive a license by:

    a. submitting the appropriate licensing fees to the Department.
    b. submitting an application to ETS.
    c. submitting an acceptable licensing application and fees to the Department.
    d. waiting for the Department to automatically send out a license.

11. In order to qualify for a nonresident license, an out-of-state broker must:

    a. be licensed and maintain a place of business in a state with licensing requirements equivalent to those of Illinois.
    b. be licensed in a state bordering Illinois that has a reciprocal licensing agreement with Illinois.
    c. have been a practicing real estate broker in his or her home state for at least the two years prior to application.
    d. all of the above

12. The Department has the legal right to:

    a. censure or reprimand a licensee without a hearing.
    b. revoke or suspend the license of a registrant after notice and hearing.
    c. initiate court action for an injunction to stop violations of the Act.
    d. b and c above

13. A licensee may initiate a lawsuit to recover compensation for services rendered if:

    a. he or she had an employment contract with the principal.
    b. he or she was a registered broker or salesperson at the time of employment.
    c. the service he or she performed was not prohibited by the Act.
    d. all of the above

14. An associate broker:

    a. may employ salespeople.
    b. may manage a branch office.
    c. may be employed by another associate broker.
    d. all of the above

15. Which of the following activities require(s) a real estate license?

    a. a resident manager collecting rent for a building owner
    b. being in the business of finding renters for apartment buildings
    c. a not-for-profit real estate referral service
    d. all of the above

16. A real estate broker's license can be revoked for many causes. Which of the following is a cause for revocation?

    a. using untruthful advertising
    b. advertising in a newspaper by a blind ad that does not give the broker's name or a properly registered assumed name
    c. depositing escrow money in his or her own personal bank account
    d. all of the above

17. Stu and Dana want to get real estate licenses. They:

   I. cannot get a license until they are 21.
   II. will get their licenses if they apply within one year of the date they pass the ETS exam.

   a. I only   c. both I and II
   b. II only   d. neither I nor II

18. Broker Liston Huzler wants to list Sara Holmes's property but is getting a lot of competition from other brokers who would also like to list the property. Huzler offers to buy the property if he doesn't sell the listing in 60 days. Huzler:

   I. can buy the property at the agreed guarantee figure and not bother advertising or using the multiple listing service as he does for other listings.
   II. must enter into a written guarantee contract signed by him and the sellers.

   a. I only   c. both I and II
   b. II only   d. neither I nor II

19. Samuel Johnson bought an apartment building through the brokerage firm of Radner and Company and hired Radner to manage the building for him. If he obtains Johnson's written consent, Radner may:

   a. post a For Rent sign on the building.
   b. use display banners to promote the apartments.
   c. advertise the property in the classified section.
   d. all of the above

20. Salesperson Jackson placed the following order with the telephone company: "List my name under 'Real Estate' as Alberta Jackson, Real Estate Salesperson, Residential Property a Specialty, 685-4107." She should have included:

   a. the expiration date of her license.
   b. her street address.
   c. the name of her employing broker.
   d. all of the above

21. While making a listing presentation, broker Kevin must be carrying:

   a. his pocket card.
   b. his sponsor card.
   c. his license.
   d. all of the above

22. Anita agrees in writing to give her cousin Mike a commission equal to half a month's rent if he finds her a tenant for the upstairs of her two-flat. Mike may sue Anita for his commission if he finds an acceptable tenant and:

   I. he holds a valid real estate license.
   II. the tenant abides by the lease for its full term.

   a. I only
   b. II only
   c. both I and II
   d. neither I nor II

15

Real Estate Financing

MORTGAGE FORMS USED

In Illinois, real property may be used to secure a debt through the use of a mortgage or a trust deed, sometimes called a deed of trust. (See Chapter 15 of the text for an explanation of each of these instruments.)

Because such forms are worded in much the same way as deeds, they appear to convey title to the mortgagee or trustee. Actually, the conveyance by the terms of the mortgage or trust deed is subject to the defeasance clause and must be reconveyed, or released back, to the mortgagor upon the payment of the debt for which the real property was put up as security. Thus, <u>Illinois does not adhere strictly to either the title or lien theory and is often referred to as an intermediary state</u>. However, <u>the mortgagor remains the owner of the mortgaged real estate</u> and holds a fee simple estate or other interest subject to the lien created by the mortgage or trust deed.

USURY

There is no limit on the rate of interest that a lender may charge a borrower in Illinois. The usury law has been temporarily suspended.

TAX RESERVE FUNDS

Lenders usually ask that certain reserves be on deposit to cover taxes and other costs that must be paid when billed. RESPA provides rules covering these reserves (also known as an escrow or impound account).

Normally the mortgagor (owner) pays 1/12th of the amount of the most recent tax bill into the fund every month and makes up for any shortage at the time the new tax bill arrives for payment by the lender. Some lenders offer alternatives to this procedure. Sometimes when the borrower places an amount in a pledged account in accordance with the lender's terms and in an amount sufficient to cover any future tax bill, he or she may not have to make monthly payments and may receive interest on the deposit. Lenders' requirements vary. Some may want one and one-half to two times the amount of the last tax to be in the account. When tax bills come, the borrower must pay from other funds and not disturb the pledged interest-bearing account.

FORECLOSURE AND REDEMPTION

If the mortgagor is in default under the terms of the mortgage or trust deed, it is necessary for the mortgagee to file a foreclosure suit in court in order to enforce the lien and have the real estate sold by a decree of the court. Before the foreclosure sale is held, the borrower may exercise his or her historical <u>equitable right</u> of redemption, i.e., pay delinquencies, penalties, and attorney fees.

Once the property is sold, the delinquent borrower has six months to redeem per his or her <u>statutory right</u> of redemption. Other defendants or others who had claims against the property may redeem too, provided they have not waived their rights. If the property has not been redeemed when the period expires, the purchaser of the property at the foreclosure sale is entitled to a deed executed by the sheriff or other officer who conducted the sale.

REAL ESTATE SECURITIES REGISTRATION

Sales of shares in partnerships or corporations can be made only under controlled conditions. To provide for the regulation and supervision of the sale of such investments to the public, securities must be registered under the laws of the federal government as well as the state. Popularly termed "Blue Sky Laws," they define under what conditions securities may be offered, sold, or purchased. In Illinois, "The Illinois Securities Law of 1953 as amended" governs.

All securities must be registered prior to sale, except for special exempt cases, which may be registered later, or which may be totally exempt. Material information regarding any offerings must be fully disclosed by a prospectus. A prospectus is defined as any communication of any offer of securities for sale, whether written or oral. Included are booklets, notices, circulars, advertisements, letters, and offers on radio or television. Radio and TV scripts must be filed and approved by the Securities Division of the Secretary of State as early as reasonably possible, but not less than 24 hours prior to broadcast.

Most offerings must be submitted to the Securities Department of the Secretary of State before they may be presented to the public. Preliminary prospectuses, exhibits, papers, and documents usually must accompany the application for registration.

There is an extensive list of requirements to which all formal printed prospectuses must adhere. Foremost among them is the printing of statements on the outside front cover in bold roman-type capital letters, as specified in the following excerpt from the law:

> **Rule 424. Statement Required in Prospectuses.**
>
> A. There shall be set forth on the outside front cover page of every prospectus the following statement in capital letters printed in boldface roman type at least as large as 10-point modern type and at least 2 points leaded:
>
> > THESE SECURITIES HAVE NOT BEEN APPROVED OR DISAPPROVED BY THE SECRETARY OF STATE OF ILLINOIS OR THE STATE OF ILLINOIS, NOR HAS THE SECRETARY OF STATE OF ILLINOIS OR THE STATE OF ILLINOIS PASSED UPON THE ACCURACY OR ADEQUACY OF THIS PROSPECTUS. ANY REPRESENTATION TO THE CONTRARY IS A CRIMINAL OFFENSE.
>
> or in the alternative, where applicable:
>
> > THESE SECURITIES HAVE NOT BEEN APPROVED OR DISAPPROVED BY THE SECURITIES AND EXCHANGE COMMISSION NOR HAS THE COMMISSION PASSED UPON THE ACCURACY OR ADEQUACY OF THIS PROSPECTUS. ANY REPRESENTATION TO THE CONTRARY IS A CRIMINAL OFFENSE.

While all securities must be registered, there are some that are exempt from the law (Section 3) and others that may be exempted from the requirement of prior registration (Section 4). Section 4 permits the filing of a report of sale no later than 30 days after the first sale of shares offered to 70 persons or less in any 12 consecutive months. There may be sales to not more than 35 persons unless the total aggregate of sales is no more than $50,000. Commissions paid may not exceed 15 percent of the initial offering price.

QUESTIONS

1. Jim and Barb Schaun arrange for a mortgage to cover their home purchase. Which of the following statements are true?

    I. Schauns may earn no interest on their funds which were impounded to cover taxes.
    II. Schauns may get interest on funds set aside to guarantee taxes will be paid when due.

    a. I only
    b. II only
    c. both I and II
    d. neither I nor II

2. Steve Perri and his wife Beverly buy shares in a new limited partnership being formed to purchase a small shopping center in Schaumburg, Illinois. Which of the following apply?

   I. They should ask for a copy of the prospectus and study it before investing.
   II. The TV ad they saw explaining the offering must be filed and approved by the Securities Division before it is shown.

   a. I only
   b. II only
   c. both I and II
   d. neither I nor II

3. Illinois real estate subject to a mortgage loan that is in default may be redeemed:

   a. by the defaulting borrower before the foreclosure sale by paying any delinquent payments and penalties.
   b. by the defaulting borrower after the foreclosure sale by redemption during the statutory period.
   c. by other persons named as defendants in the foreclosure suit by redemption during the statutory period.
   d. by all of the above

4. All regulated securities:

   a. are recorded by the Illinois Department of Registration and Education.
   b. are controlled under the Illinois usury law.
   c. must be registered with the Secretary of State of Illinois.
   d. a and b above

5. In Illinois, real estate pledged as security for a mortgage loan:

   a. belongs to the lender until the debt is paid in full, although the borrower has the right to use the property.
   b. is released to the borrower when the debt is paid in full.
   c. is not secured through use of a trust deed.
   d. a and b above

6. If agreed to by their lender, mortgage borrowers may deposit monies equal to 1/12th of the yearly real estate taxes into their checking accounts each month:

   a. as an alternative to paying into a separate tax reserve fund.
   b. to assure the statutory right of redemption against possible acceleration and foreclosure.
   c. to avoid prepayment penalties.
   d. none of the above

7. Under federal law, the Federal National Mortgage Association (Fannie Mae) may:

    a. purchase FHA and VA loans.
    b. buy conventional loans.
    c. sell loans to institutions.
    d. all of the above

8. Tom Clark signed a $10,000 note secured by a second mortgage on his home. The term of the loan was for five years and monthly payments of $125, including 9 1/2 percent interest, were required. Which of the following statements is true?

    a. Clark had a fully amortized second mortgage loan.
    b. Clark had signed a note with a balloon payment required.
    c. This was an example of a straight payment plan mortgage loan.
    d. This was probably a flexible payment plan, but not enough information is given in the question.

9. The Baronis obtained a first mortgage loan of $50,000 at 9.6 percent interest. Monthly payments of $615 include $114 set aside for taxes. Twenty-six dollars is reserved for homeowners insurance. If the balance of the payment is credited first to interest and then to principal, what is the loan balance after the first payment?

    a. $49,600
    b. $49,740
    c. $49,925
    d. $49,950

16

Leases

In Illinois the term lease includes any "letting," whether by verbal or written agreement. However, no court action can be brought on a lease for a term of more than one year that is not in writing and signed by both parties or their authorized agents.

LEASE PROVISIONS

Lessor Liability for Negligence

Any lease provision stating that lessors are exempt from liability for monetary damages resulting from injuries to persons or property caused by the negligence of the lessor, his or her agents, servants or employees, in the operation or maintenance of the leased premises is void and unenforceable, but does not render the entire contract void. This law applies to all forms of leases: land, industrial, and commercial, as well as residential.

Tenants' Complaint of Code Violations

Any lease provision or any understanding purporting to give a landlord the right to terminate or refuse to renew a lease on the ground that the tenant has complained to any governmental authority about a bona fide violation of a building code, health ordinance, or similar regulation, is considered to be against public policy and is void, but does not render the entire lease void.

Recording

Creditors of the property owner and purchasers who do not have actual notice of the terms of the particular lease are charged with legal notice of the lease on and after the date on which it is filed for record in the County Recorder's Office. However, the premises should be inspected and the interest of the parties in possession should be determined. Actual possession by the tenant under an unrecorded lease is notice of his or her rights.

Interest on Security Rent Deposits

Landlords who receive security deposits on residential leases of units in properties of 25 or more units at the same location are required to pay interest at the rate of <u>5 percent per year, from the date of the deposit, on any deposit held for more than six months</u>. Interest may be paid in cash or credit on the rent, except when the lessee is in default. Furthermore, recent Illinois law imposes a penalty on landlords who withhold required payment of interest on security deposits. Any property owner who is found by a court to be willfully withholding such security deposit interest must pay the tenant an amount equal to the security deposit plus the tenant's court costs and attorney's fees.

Rent Concessions

A rent concession is a reduction or abatement in the established rent granted by the landlord to induce the tenant to enter into the lease. It may be based on services to be rendered by the tenant or it may be the result of a poor rental market. To protect prospective purchasers and/or lenders, Illinois law requires that if a rent concession is given in any lease, except for farm property, the lessor must place across the face and text of the lease the words "Concession Granted." A notation on the margin should state the nature of the concession. Failure to do this subjects the lessor to penalties under the law.

TERMINATION OF TENANCY

Leases may be terminated by the expiration of the lease period, mutual agreement of the parties, or breach of a lease provision by either landlord or tenant as explained in Chapter 16 of the text.

Expiration of Lease (Estates for Years)

When a written lease establishes an expiration date, the tenant is obligated to surrender possession upon the termination date. No notice or demand by the lessor is necessary to terminate the lease. However, owners and managers of any rental property should always question tenants with expiring leases a reasonable time before the end of the lease period to allow themselves time to replace vacating tenants.

Notice to Terminate (Periodic Estates)

1. <u>Tenancy from year to year</u>. The landlord must give the tenant 60 days' written notice within a period six months to 60 days prior to the termination of the tenancy.

2. <u>Tenancy from month to month</u>. If the tenant holds over without special agreement, the landlord must give the tenant 30 days' written notice to terminate.

3. **Tenancy from week to week.** If the tenant holds over without special agreement, the landlord must give the tenant seven days' written notice to terminate.

4. **Farm tenancies from year to year.** The landlord is usually required to give the tenant four months' written notice to terminate.

After an estate for years is terminated on the expiration date, or a periodic estate is terminated by proper notice, no further demand by the landlord is necessary, and he or she may immediately bring suit for possession (see Suit for Possession).

After Default

When a tenant defaults in any of the terms of a lease including failure to pay rent, the lease may be terminated by ten-day written notice setting forth the nature of the default and demanding possession. A ten-day notice allows the landlord to demand possession even if the fault is corrected. This notice, signed by the lessor, can be delivered to the tenant either in person or to anyone over the age of ten years residing on the premises, or by certified or registered mail with a return receipt, or by posting the notice on the premises if no one is in actual possession.

When a tenant defaults only in payment of rent, the landlord may elect to serve the tenant with a five-day notice, which demands payment of the delinquent rent within a five-day period. Failure to pay the delinquent rent after receiving the notice will allow the landlord to terminate the lease and sue for possession. However, if the delinquent rent is paid, the lease will then continue in force.

Suit for Possession (Eviction)

After proper notice of the termination of a tenancy, the landlord may proceed with a suit for "forcible entry and detainer" to obtain judgment for possession. When the court rules in favor of the landlord, a "writ of restitution" will be issued, which may be delivered to a bailiff who will forcibly evict the tenant. The landlord may also include in the suit a claim for any rent due, which is called a "joint action."

In Illinois, a landlord has no right to "self help"; that is, he or she may not forcibly remove a tenant without following court procedures as provided by state law.

QUESTIONS

1. In Illinois, a lease for more than one year:

    a. must be in writing and signed by the lessor and lessee or their authorized agents.
    b. must include a provision for interest to be paid on all security deposits.
    c. must be recorded to give notice of the resident tenant's right of possession.
    d. must be terminated by written notice to the tenant if it contains a definite expiration date.

2. Marsha Tubman rents an apartment in a 100-unit high rise in Chicago for $300 per month. Tubman decides to move when she learns that her rent will be raised by 50 percent at the expiration of her one-year lease. When she moved in, Tubman deposited $300 as security deposit. How much interest on the deposit will Tubman receive when she moves out if no money is subtracted for damages?

    a. $30
    b. $18
    c. $15
    d. $21

3. Norm Davis agrees to rent the ground floor apartment to Edgar Springs at 7 percent off the $185 per month regular rent in return for repair work Springs will do on the building.

    a. After one year Springs will have saved $155.40 on his rent.
    b. The lease between the parties is void.
    c. The parties must sign a separate rent concession agreement and record it.
    d. none of the above.

4. Tenancies from month to month may be terminated upon advance notice of:

    a. one week.
    b. five days.
    c. 30 days.
    d. 60 days.

5. Patricia Owens lives in a large Illinois housing project subsidized by HUD. She rents her apartment on a one-year lease at $130 per month. Owens is repeatedly in arrears on her rent. At present she is one month behind in her rent and the landlord wants to evict her. What can the landlord do?

   a. Under the Tenant's Eviction Procedures Act, the landlord must give Owens two months' notice.
   b. The landlord may sue to evict Owens after giving 10 days' written notice.
   c. The landlord must petition HUD before he can evict Owens.
   d. a and c above

6. Landlord Allen leases an apartment to Martha Ross and provides in the written lease that Ms. Ross's lease can be terminated if she reports any building code violations to the city. This provision:

   a. exempts the lessor from liability for damages for injury to persons caused by the condition of the building.
   b. can be enforced in court as it is a written provision in a properly signed lease contract.
   c. makes the entire lease void.
   d. none of the above

7. Landlord H, who owns a 25-unit apartment building in Decatur, Illinois, has held tenant Q's security deposit for three months. At the end of three months Q, who is on a month-to-month lease, informs H that he desires to move after 30 days. Which statement is true?

   a. H will have to pay Q an interest of 5 percent on his security deposit.
   b. H owes Q no interest on his security deposit.
   c. Q is entitled to 6 percent interest on his security deposit.
   d. Q cannot legally move after 30 days.

8. Fred Carroll leases an apartment from Lake Shore Realty form May 1, 1982, to April 30, 1983, with a monthly rent payment of $210. If Carroll fails to pay his apartment rent when due, the landlord can:

   a. serve notice on Carroll to pay the delinquent rent wihin five days.
   b. serve Carroll with a notice that the lease will terminate in ten days.
   c. evict the tenant by hiring a mover to take away his furniture and personal property.
   d. a and b above

9. Carol Burtois has a one-year lease in a 12-unit apartment building. What can happen if she has a lease that expires May 31?

   I. Carol will receive five percent interest on her security deposit because it was held more than six months.
  II. She must vacate the premises by June 1, even if owner doesn't ask.

      a. I only   c. both I and II
      b. II only   d. neither I nor II

19/20

Control Of Land Use/Subdividing and Property Development

ENABLING LEGISLATION AND PENALTIES

The statutes of all states, including Illinois, embody laws that confer zoning powers to local governments such as counties, cities, and villages. These laws are called enabling acts. There are no statewide zoning laws in Illinois or any other state. The authority of each state to allow local governments to regulate zoning derives from the 14th Amendment to the U.S. Constitution, which grants each state the right to pass laws for protecting the health, safety, and general welfare of its citizens. Local governments may penalize violators of their zoning laws; in Illinois, such penalties generally consist of fines and/or injunctions.

HOME RULE

The 1970 Illinois Constitution provides home rule--local self-government for any municipality with a population in excess of 25,000 or for any county whose chief executive officer is elected by the people of the county. These home rule cities and counties have greater police power than other districts; an ordinance may include the penalty of a jail sentence not to exceed six months. However, home rule units do not generally prescribe jail sentences as penalties; although, if in addition to the fine an injunction is issued and then violated, the violator may be held in contempt of court and sentenced to jail.

The Illinois Constitution provides that, when a conflict occurs between a home rule city and a home rule county, the city ordinance prevails within its jurisdiction.

ILLINOIS LAND SALES ACT

The sale or promotion within Illinois of subdivided land located outside the state is regulated by the Illinois Land Sales Act. The Act, which is administered by the Department of Registration and Education, regulates the offering, sale, lease, or assignment of any improved or unimproved land divided into 50 or more lots and offered as part of a common promotional plan. The Act does not apply to land purchased in a single transaction by one person for his or her own account; to land with a building on it, or contracted for a building within two years; to land for use as cemetery lots; to subdivided land being sold to less than 11 people; or to parcels of 20 or more unimproved acres or ten or more acres with access leading to county-maintained roads.

Under the Act, subdividers must register with the Department of Registration and Education, providing full information on the land, location, tax status, financial arrangements, and liens associated with the offering. Similar information must be included in a public property report approved by the Department. This report must be given to all prospective purchasers of the offering. A purchaser who does not receive a copy of this report at least 48 hours before signing a binding contract of sale has the option of avoiding the contract within 48 hours of signing.

The Department has the right to investigate every subdivision submitted for registration, including on-site inspection at the expense of the applicant or searches of records held by other state or federal agencies. If, after registration, the Department determines that fraudulent statements or misrepresentation have been used in the offering, advertising, or sale of the subdivided land, it may rule against the subdivider and give him or her seven days to answer the complaint. Upon failure to answer, the Department may issue a cease and desist order prohibiting a hearing to revoke or suspend the subdivider's certificate of registration. Violations of the Act are also punishable by the courts, which may assess fines and/or imprisonment.

Anyone in the business of selling out-of-state subdivided land from offices within Illinois must be a licensed Illinois real estate broker. However, a person who sells out-of-state subdivided land in Illinois without entering the state does not need an Illinois license.

QUESTIONS

1. Enabling legislation in Illinois:

    a. grants counties, cities, and villages the power to make and enforce local zoning ordinances.
    b. makes all counties, cities, and villages subject to Illinois state zoning laws.
    c. requires all Illinois counties, cities, and villages to adopt the requirements of the federal municipal planning commission.
    d. sets environmental controls on current land use.

2. The Illinois Land Sales Act:

    a. regulates the sale of all subdivided land located in Illinois.
    b. applies to the sale or lease of both Illinois and out-of-state unimproved land.
    c. requires the subdivider to procure a certificate of registration from the Department of Registration and Education before offering out-of-state subdivided property for sale to persons in Illinois.
    d. all of the above

3. Sherry Scrattish wants her town in Illinois zoned to prohibit video game arcades. She should:

    a. try to get a change in the Illinois state zoning laws.
    b. file suit to force the town to conform with Illinois zoning laws.
    c. try to persuade her town government to change its zoning laws.
    d. appeal to the U.S. Department of Housing and Urban Development.

21

Fair Housing Laws and Ethical Practices

The Illinois Real Estate License Act and its General Rules require that all licensees in Illinois must fully adhere to the principles of equal opportunity in housing.

Section 18 of the License Act expressly prohibits the following discriminatory acts:

> Influencing or attempting to influence by any words or acts a prospective seller, purchaser, occupant, landlord or tenant of real estate, in connection with viewing, buying or leasing of real estate, so as to promote, or tend to promote, the continuance or maintenance of racially and religiously segregated housing, or so as to retard, obstruct or discourage racially integrated housing on or in any street, block, neighborhood, or community.

In addition, Section 18 prohibits any act that violates those sections of the Illinois Human Rights Act reprinted below, whether or not a complaint has been filed with or adjudicated by the Human Rights Commission.

Section 3-102. *Civil Rights Violations: Real Estate Transactions*

It is a civil rights violation for an owner or any other person engaging in a real estate transaction, or for a real estate broker or salesman, because of unlawful discrimination, to

(A) *Transaction.* Refuse to engage in a real estate transaction with a person;

(B) *Terms.* Alter the terms, conditions or privileges of a real estate transaction or in the furnishing of facilities or services in connection therewith;

(C) *Offer.* Refuse to receive or to fail to transmit a bona fide offer to engage in a real estate transaction from a person;

(D) *Negotiation.* Refuse to negotiate for a real estate transaction with a person.

(E) *Representations.* Represent to a person that real property is not available for inspection, sale, rental, or lease when in fact it is so available, or to fail to bring a property listing to his or her attention, or to refuse to permit him or her to inspect real property;

(F) *Publication of Intent.* Print, circulate, post, mail, publish, or cause to be so published a written or oral statement, advertisement or sign, or to use a form of application for a real estate transaction, or to make a record or inquiry in connection with a prospective real estate transaction, which expresses any limitation founded upon, or indicates, directly or indirectly, an intent to engage in unlawful discrimination;

(G) *Listings.* Offer, solicit, accept, use or retain a listing of real property with knowledge that unlawful discrimination in a real estate transaction is intended.

Section 3-103. *Blockbusting*

It is a civil rights violation for any person to:

(A) *Solicitation.* Solicit for sale, lease, listing or purchase any residential real estate within this State, on the grounds of loss of value due to the present or prospective entry into the vicinity of the property involved of any person or persons of any particular race, color, religion, national origin, ancestry, age, sex, marital status or handicap.

(B) *Statements.* Distribute or cause to be distributed, written material or statements designed to induce any owner of residential real estate in the State to sell or lease his or her property because of any present or prospective changes in the race, color, religion, national origin, ancestry, age, sex, marital status or handicap of residents in the vicinity of the property involved.

(C) *Creating Alarm.* Intentionally create alarm, among residents of any community, by transmitting communications in any manner, including a telephone call whether or not conversation thereby ensues, with a design to induce any owner of residential real estate in this state to sell or lease his or her property because of any present or prospective entry into the vicinity of the property involved of any person or persons of any particular race, color, religion, national origin, ancestry, age, sex, marital status or handicap.

Section 3-104. *Exclusion of Children in the Rental of Real Estate*

It is a civil rights violation for the owner or agent of any housing accommodation to:

(A) Require, as a condition precedent to the rental of a housing accommodation, that the prospective tenant shall not have, at the time the application for rental is made, one or more children under the age of 14 years residing in his or her family; or

(B) Insert in any lease or agreement for the rental of any housing accommodation a condition terminating the lease if there shall be one or more children under the age of 14 in the family of any person holding the lease and occupying the housing accommodation.

Section 3-104.1. *Refusal to sell or rent because a person has a guide or hearing dog. It is a civil rights violation for the owner or agent of any housing accommodation to:*

(A) refuse to sell or rent after the making of a bonafide offer, or to refuse to negotiate for the sale or rental of, or otherwise make unavailable or deny property to any blind or hearing impaired person because he has a guide or hearing dog: or

(B) discriminate against any blind or hearing impaired person in the terms, conditions, or privileges of sale or rental property, or in the provision of services or facilities in connection therewith, because he has a guide or hearing dog: or

(C) require, because a blind or hearing impaired person has a guide or hearing dog, an extra charge in a lease, rental agreement, or contract of purchase or sale, other than for actual damage done to the premises by the dog.

Any agreement or lease which contains a condition of the type described in this Section is void as to that condition.

Section 3-105. *Restrictive Covenants*

(A) *Agreements.* Every provision in an oral agreement or a written instrument relating to real property which purports to forbid or restrict the conveyance, encumbrance, occupancy or lease thereof on the basis of race, color, religion, or national origin is void.

(B) *Limitations.* (1) Every condition, restriction or prohibition, including a right of entry or possibility of reverter, which directly or indirectly limits the use or occupancy of real property on the basis of race, color, religion, or national origin is void.

(2) This Section shall not apply to a limitation of use on the basis of religion of real property held by a religious institution or organization or by a religious or charitable organization operated, supervised, or controlled by a religious institution or organization, and used for religious or charitable purposes.

(C) *Civil Rights Violations.* It is a civil rights violation to insert in a written instrument relating to real property a provision that is void under this Section or to honor or attempt to honor such a provision in the chain of title.

Section 3-106. *Exemptions*

Nothing contained in Section 3-102 shall prohibit:

(A) *Private Sales of Single Family Homes.* Any sale of a single family home by its owner so long as the following criteria are met:

(1) The owner does not own or have a beneficial interest in more than three single family homes at the time of the sale;

(2) The owner or a member of his or her family was the last current resident of the home;

(3) The home is sold without the use in any manner of the sales or rental facilities or services of any real estate broker or salesman, or of any employee or agent of any real estate broker or salesman;

(4) The home is sold without the publication, posting or mailing, after notice, of any advertisement or written notice in violation of paragraph (F) of Section 3-102.

(B) *Apartments.* Rental of a housing accommodation in a building which contains housing accommodations for not more than five families living independently of each other, if the lessor or a member of his or her family resides in one of the housing accommodations;

(C) *Private Rooms.* Rental of a room or rooms in a private home by an owner if he or she or a member of his or her family resides therein or, while absent for a period of not more than twelve months, if he or she or a member of his or her family intends to return to reside therein;

(D) *Government Supported Housing Programs.* Restricting rental or sale of a housing accommodation to a person of a certain age group when such housing accommodation is authorized, approved, financed or subsidized in whole or in part, for the benefit of that age group, by a unit of state, local or federal government.

(E) *Religious Organizations.* A religious organization, association, or society, or any nonprofit institution or organization operated, supervised or controlled by or in conjunction with a religious organization, association, or society, from limiting the sale, rental or occupancy of a dwelling which it owns or operates for other than a commerical purpose to persons of the same religion, or from giving preference to such persons, unless membership in such religion is restricted on account of race, color, or national origin.

(F) *Sex.* Restricting the rental of rooms in a housing accommodation to persons of one sex.

In addition to the provisions contained in the Licensing Act, the General Rules of the Act prohibit a licensed broker or salesperson from taking any listing or participating in any transaction where the owner of the property seeks to apply discriminatory standards (General Rule X). Violations of the provisions or restrictions of the Act or the Rules can result in the revocation, suspension, or nonrenewal of the violator's license by the Department as discussed in Chapter 14. Also, the Department may censure, reprimand, or impose a civil penalty not to exceed $10,000.

Federal and Local Laws

Equal opportunity in housing is guaranteed to all United States residents under the Civil Rights Act of 1866 and the Federal Fair Housing Act of 1968 as discussed in the text.

In addition to state and federal laws, many cities and villages in Illinois have fair housing laws which in some cases are equal to the federal fair housing law. These laws are enforced on the local level and, as noted in the text, action under these laws may take precedence over federal laws when the local law has been ruled substantially equivalent to the federal statute.

QUESTIONS

1. Salesperson Bob has a listing on an owner-occupied single-family house in the city. He will be committing a civil rights violation if he:

    I. refuses offers from everyone who is not of European descent.
    II. advertises the property as for "Asians only."

    a. I only
    b. II only
    c. both I and II
    d. neither I nor II

2. Rose and Pete decide to sell their house, their only real property, without help from a broker. They will move out and go to Wisconsin as soon as the house is sold. They will commit a civil rights violation if they:

    I. advertise the property as for "Germans only."
    II. refuse offers from anyone not of German descent.

    a. I only
    b. II only
    c. both I and II
    d. neither I nor II

110   ILLINOIS SUPPLEMENT for Modern Real Estate Practice

3. Kevin just bought an apartment building with three units. His deed contains an agreement that he will not rent to anyone who is not black. This provision:

   I. renders Kevin's deed void.
  II. cannot be enforced.

   a. I only   c. both I and II
   b. II only   d. neither I nor II

4. In the situation in Question 3, Kevin decides to abide by the provision as described. Who has committed a civil rights violation?

   I. Kevin
  II. the former owner who inserted the provision

   a. I only   c. both I and II
   b. II only   d. neither I nor II

5. The Illinois License Act prohibits discrimination in the form of:

   a. volunteering information concerning the sex, creed, physical or mental handicap, race, color, religion, or ethnic composition of a community.
   b. attempting to influence the sale, lease, or viewing of real estate in an effort to maintain segregated housing.
   c. refusing to list, sell, or show real estate because of sex, creed, physical or mental handicap, race, color, religion, or national origin of the prospective clients or because of the composition of the neighborhood where the property is located.
   d. all of the above

6. Blockbusting:

   a. plays upon homeowners' fears of rapid change in the ethnic or racial composition of their neighborhood, frequently resulting in panic selling.
   b. if proven, results in a reprimand against the broker responsible but is not grounds for revocation of a real estate license in Illinois.
   c. applies only to selling, not leasing, of residential property.
   d. all of the above

7. Salesperson Ron White gets the listing for Sean Popski's house, but only on the condition that there will be "no dumb Canadians comin' round." Which of the following actions are permitted or required by law?

   I. He can take the listing, but must explain to Popski that he will show the property to all qualified and interested buyers.
   II. He must refuse the listing if Popski insists on his conditions.

   a. I only
   b. II only
   c. both I and II
   d. neither I nor II

23

Closing the Real Estate Transaction

CLOSING PROCEDURES

A real estate sales transaction is completed or closed according to the terms of the sales contract executed by the buyer and the seller. The closing process invloves three main areas of activity: (1) The seller shows evidence of ownership such as a title insurance policy, Torrens certificate, abstract and attorney's opinion, or other proof of title, as required by the sales contract; the buyer is required to pay the balance due on the purchase only after the seller presents title evidence corresponding to those requirements. (2) A closing statement showing the net amounts owed by the buyer and due to the seller must be prepared. (3) The actual delivery of the seller's deed and the payment of monies owed by the buyer is conducted at the buyer's mortgage lender, at the broker's office, through an escrow agent, or in any other manner prescribed in the sales contract.

Preparation of Closing Statements

All licensed persons must be aware of the following two provisions in regard to the preparation of closing statements.

General Rule XIII issued by the Department of Registration and Education for the administration of the License Act reads as follows:

> Real estate brokers or associate brokers shall prepare closing statements only regarding funds coming into their possession or control, except at the direction of attorneys to the transaction. Generally the closing statements prepared by a broker or associate broker will cover disposition of earnest money only.

PRORATIONS

In Illinois, prorations or apportionments are drawn up to, and including, the day of closing. In practice, therefore, this means that the day of closing is considered to be a day of expense as well as a day of income for the seller.

114   ILLINOIS SUPPLEMENT for Modern Real Estate Practice

Three acceptable methods may be used in computing prorations:

1. Actual Number of Days. Prorations by this procedure are calculated by dividing the annual charge to be prorated by 365 days (366 days during leap year). The daily amount is then multiplied by the actual number of days chargeable to the seller.

    For example, if the tax proration were to include March 5 (the day of closing), the total number of days would be 64 (or 65), computed as follows: January, 31; February, 28 (or 29); March, 5.

2. Statutory Month. Under this method, the yearly amount is divided by 12 to determine the monthly amount and the monthly figure is divided by 30 to find the daily amount.

3. Sample Rules for Closing Real Estate Sales are reproduced in Chapter 23 of Modern Real Estate Practice. Under this method, the number of days in the month of closing is used in calculating the per diem proration.

    In the tax example shown in 1 above, two months would be 2/12ths of the annual amount and five days would be 5/31sts of the monthly amount. The per diem expense for the five days in this example is calculated on a 31-day month basis because March has 31 days.

Assumed mortgages. In Illinois the terms of some mortgage loans provide that interest is charged at the beginning of the month (in advance); without this provision, interest is charged at the end of the month (in arrears). When the interest on an existing mortgage to be assumed by the buyer is charged at the beginning of the month, the unearned portion (that is, the portion that is prepaid from the date of closing to the end of the month) must be credited to the seller, and debited to the buyer. When the mortgage interest is charged at the end of the month, the earned portion of the mortgage interest through the date of closing is an accrued expense (a debit) to the seller and is credited to the buyer.

Taxes. In Illinois there may be two kinds of taxes to be considered at the closing: general real estate taxes and special assessments. The general tax is charged by the calendar year and is prorated. Special assessments are usually due and payable on January 2 of each year. Whoever owns the property on this date is usually responsible for paying this entire installment. However, this practice can be altered by an agreement between buyer and seller. When a buyer assumes payment of the future installments of a special assessment, the contract may provide that the prorations are to include a credit to buyer for interest accrued from January 2 to date of closing on the unpaid balance of the special assessment.

Wages. Building employee wages accrued from the last wage period through the day of closing are an expense of the seller and are credited to the purchaser. Under certain circumstances, a janitor who is a member of the Flat Janitors' Union is entitled to an annual paid vacation and the accrued vacation allowance, through the day of closing, is credited to the purchaser. The Chicago Area Agreement provides that the vacation year is computed from June 1 through the date of closing.

For example: the janitor receives $1,440 monthly wages payable at the end of the month and the sale is to be closed on the 10th of April. $1,440 ÷ 30 =

23/Closing the Real Estate Transaction   115

$48 per day X 10 days = $480 proration credited to the buyer. The local employment rules allow this janitor a paid vacation of two weeks, which is computed as representing 46 percent of a month's wages:

$1,440	X	46 percent	=	$662.40
$662.40	÷	12 months	=	$ 55.20 per month
$55.20	÷	30 days	=	$ 1.839 per day

The proration is from June 1 to and including April 10 and equals ten months and ten days.

$55.20	X	10 months	=	$552.00
$ 1.839	X	10 days	=	18.39
		Total proration to buyer		$570.39

State transfer tax stamps required on deeds are explained in <u>Supplement</u> Chapter 12.

All other proration rules set forth in Chapter 23 of the text are applicable in Illinois. The rules entitled "Accrued Items and Prepaid Items" also apply in Illinois. (Note that rental security deposits held by the seller under the lease terms are not prorated and are credited in total to the purchaser.)

<u>ESCROWS</u>

Some transactions in Illinois are closed in escrow, as explained in text Chapters 11 and 23.

<u>CLOSING PROBLEM</u>

Now that you have learned the procedures for preparing a closing statement, you will have the opportunity to use them. The problem is similar to the one that will appear on the Illinois Real Estate Broker's Examination.

<u>Data Describing the Real Estate Transaction</u>

Tom Archer, a salesperson for the Arrow Real Estate Company, which is a member of the local multiple listing service, secured a 120-day exclusive-right-to-sell listing on September 13, 1983, from Ryan and Erin Bowman.

The listing was for their home at 811 Stowell Drive, Palatine, Illinois 60067 (Cook County).

The house is a two-story colonial with a full basement. It contains 1,300 square feet of floor space. The first floor includes a living room, 18 feet by 15 feet; a dining room, 12 feet by 12 feet; a kitchen with breakfast space, 18 feet by 12 feet; and a tiled powder room. The second floor includes three bedrooms with two full baths; the bedrooms measure 20 feet by 12 feet, 14 feet by 12 feet and 11 feet by 10 feet. The basement has a paneled recreation

116   ILLINOIS SUPPLEMENT for Modern Real Estate Practice

room, 22 feet by 18 feet, and a laundry room, 10 feet by 9 feet; there is a forced hot air gas-fired furnace and an electric water heater. City water and sewer services are provided, and the house uses natural gas. There is no attic.

The house was built in 1965; it is of brick construction, and has an attached two-car garage with a paved side drive. The lot measures 60 feet by 150 feet, and the legal description is lot 12, block Q of the Parkview subdivision, as taken from a deed to the Bowmans that is recorded in Book 503, Page 6. The Bowmans own the property in fee, and they have agreed to include the gas cooking range, the electric refrigerator, the gas clothes dryer and the electric washer in the total selling price of $127,500. Sellers agree to furnish a termite inspection.

The First Federal Bank of Woodland holds a mortgage on the property with an unpaid balance of $53,300 as of September 1. It is an amortized or direct reduction loan. Interest is charged at the rate of 8 percent per annum, with the final payment to be made within 13 years. The bank has indicated that this mortgage may be assumed by a qualified buyer. Monthly payments of $550.63 are applied first to the interest, then to the balance of the principal.

Real estate taxes for 1982 of $1,224 have been paid. The broker's commission is to be 6 1/2 percent of the gross sales price.

On November 15, 1983, the salesperson obtained a bona fide offer from Brian and Toni Morrow to purchase the property for $123,000. The offer was on the basis of 30 percent in cash, the buyers' assumption of the balance of the existing mortgage, and the sellers taking back a purchase money mortgage for the remainder of the purchase price, to be paid over five years at 12 percent interest. The buyers agreed to assume a prepaid three-year fire and hazard insurance policy effective from noon, June 1, 1982 through noon, June 1, 1985. The sellers paid a three-year premium of $1,110. Possession was desired as of the date of closing, which was to be no later than December 15, 1983. The offer was accompanied by a check for $6,150. The sellers accepted the offer, and a contract was prepared on the basis of the Morrows' terms.

The expenses for closing this transaction also include the following:

1. Title insurance policy/sellers' share--$468, buyers' share--$80
2. Preparation of deed (sellers' expense)--$100
3. Preparation of purchase money mortgage (buyers' expense)--$100
4. Termite inspection (sellers' expense)--$50
5. Transfer tax--$.50 per $500 or fraction thereof, less assumed mortgage (sellers' expense)
6. Recording charges of $10 each for deed and purchase money mortgage (buyers' expense)--$20
7. Settlement charge for purchase money mortgage (buyers' expense)--$50

Working the Closing Problem

The settlement statement worksheet that appears on page 118 is very similar to the one that appears on the Illinois Real Estate Broker's Examination. The worksheet itself is not considered in the final examination score, but is used to answer later exam questions, so the settlement information must be filled in accurately and clearly for later use. Note that computation of the

23/Closing the Real Estate Transaction   117

settlement statement worksheet includes every expense and proration involved in the transaction, not just monies that pass between buyer and seller.

To use the worksheet most efficiently, the following steps should be followed:

1. As you read through the information given for the problem, list the titles of all charges included in the transaction in the first column of the worksheet.

2. Go through the list of charges and consider those items related to the buyer; make any necessary proration computations and record each buyer-related expense as either a debit to the buyer (an amount the buyer owes) or a credit to the buyer (an amount the buyer has already paid, promises to pay in the form of a loan or note or will be paid by him).

3. Next, go through the list of charges and consider those items related to the seller; make necessary proration computations and record each seller-related expense as either a debit to the seller (an amount the seller owes) or a credit to the seller (the selling price of the property and any prorated expenses the seller has prepaid).

4. Total the buyer's debit and credit columns, and subtract the lesser from the greater total to determine what amount the buyer must pay at the closing (if debits exceed credits).

5. Total the seller's debit and credit columns, and subtract the lesser from the greater total to determine what amount the seller will pay at the closing (if debits exceed credits) or what amount the seller will be paid at the closing (if credits exceed debits).

   To begin the problem, reread the example transaction and list all expense categories on the worksheet. Don't fill in any other columns yet.

Itemized Expenses on Settlement Statement Worksheet

At this point, you should have listed the following information in the first column of the settlement worksheet:

    Purchase price
    Earnest money deposit
    Assumed mortgage principal
    Prorated mortgage interest
    Purchase money mortgage
    Real estate tax proration
    Broker's commission
    Title insurance policy charges
    Preparation of deed charge
    Preparation of purchase money mortgage charge
    Termite inspection
    Transfer tax
    Fire and hazard insurance premium proration
    Recording fees (deed and purchase money mortgage)
    Settlement charge

SETTLEMENT STATEMENT WORKSHEET

Property _____

Seller _____

Buyer _____

Settlement Date _____

| | BUYER'S STATEMENT || SELLER'S STATEMENT ||
	DEBIT	CREDIT	DEBIT	CREDIT

23/Closing the Real Estate Transaction   119

If you left any items out, add them to the worksheet at the bottom of your list. (The order of the items is not important.) When your list is complete, work through it, considering only those expenses that affect the buyers and record the results of your computations in the proper column. Then, work through the list again, considering those expenses that affect the sellers and make those entries. Compute all prorations on the basis of a 30-day month. Work all computations to three decimal places; do not round off until you have arrived at the final proration figure.

All items are both debited to one party and credited to the other party with the exception of: earnest money; sellers' out-of-pocket expenses such as commission and title insurance; and buyers' out-of-pocket expenses such as loan origination fees.

Check all your completed entries and computations against those detailed below. In order for your answers to agree with the completed settlement statement worksheet in the Answer Key, it is important to use the expense information as it is given above; do not try to alter the data to correspond with real estate practice in your particular area.

Purchase price. A debit to the buyers because they have promised to pay in cash or otherwise account for the entire agreed-upon price of the property. A credit to the sellers because they will be reimbursed for the selling price of the property.

Earnest money deposit. The buyers have paid 5 percent of the $123,000 purchase price, or $6,150, so this amount is credited to them. (Since the $6,150 was paid to the broker, rather than the sellers, this amount is not part of the seller's statement. However, it will be included in the total money due the sellers at the closing.)

Assumed mortgage principal and interest. The unpaid balance of the sellers' mortgage was $53,300 as of September 1 (the listing was taken September 13). However, as the sale was closed on December 15, three more monthly payments were made by the sellers and the balance reduced as follows:

Date	Balance
September 1	$53,300.00
October 1	53,104.70
November 1	52,908.10
December 1	52,710.19

Therefore, the unpaid balance of the assumed mortgage on December 15 was the December 1 balance, and the prorated interest is based on that figure. Interest proration is for interest December 1 to 15 or one-half month:

$52,710.19 X 8% = $4,216.82 per year
$4,216.82 ÷ 12   = $351.40 per month
$351.40 ÷ 2   = $175.70

Since the buyers agree to assume the sellers' remaining mortgage debt, the balance of the principal remaining is credited to them, as well as the interest that accrued on that principal while the sellers had possession of the property in part of the month of December. Since the sellers are relieved of the indebtedness for both the remaining principal and the interest for that part of December in which they were in possession of the property, both amounts are debited to them. In effect, the sellers are paying off their indebtedness with part of the purchase price of the property.

Purchase money mortgage. The buyers are paying 30 percent in cash and assuming the existing mortgage. The sellers are taking back a purchase money mortgage for the remainder of the purchase price.

Purchase Price			$123,000.00
Less:	30% Cash	$36,900.00	
	Assumed Mortgage	52,710.19	89,610.19
Purchase Money Mortgage			$ 33,389.81

Since the buyers agree to pay the amount of the purchase money mortgage at a future date, that amount is credited to them. Since the sellers agree to accept part of the purchase price in the future, that part of the purchase price must be debited to them, to be subtracted from the amount they receive on the day of closing.

Real estate tax. In Illinois, real estate taxes become a lien on January 2 of the year following December 31. They are paid in arrears on June 1 and September 1 of the year after the taxable year. The sellers have paid the 1982 tax of $1,224. Since the buyers will pay 1983 taxes in 1984, the sellers must credit the buyers for the proration of this year's taxes up to December 15; that is, 11 months and 15 days.

$1,224 ÷ 12 = $102 per month
$102 ÷ 30 = $3.40 per day
$102 X 11 = $1,122
$3.40 X 15 = $51.00
$1,122 + $51 = $1,173.00

The sellers will be debited with this amount as their share of the tax and the buyers will be credited with the same amount.

Broker's commission. The sellers must pay the broker's commission rate of 6 1/2 percent of the selling price of $123,000, as agreed. Since the sellers owe the broker this amount, it is a debit to the sellers. The buyers will not pay the broker a commission.

Preparation of purchase money mortgage, recording fees for both deed and purchase money mortgage and settlement charge. As agreed, the buyers will pay these expenses, so they are debited to the buyers.

Title insurance. In Illinois, it is customary for the seller to pay for the title search, examination, and insurance; the buyer usually pays for title insurance to cover the mortgagee. In this instance the cost of the title insurance policy is $468 to the sellers and $80 to the buyers (both debits).

Fire and hazard insurance. Since the policy was prepaid, the sellers will be credited with the unearned premium:

$1,110 premium ÷ 3 years = $370.00 per year
$370.00 ÷ 12 = $30.833 per month
$30.833 ÷ 30 = $1.028 per day

23/Closing the Real Estate Transaction   121

```
     year    mo.      day

              17
     1984     5̶       31
     1̶9̶8̶5̶     6̶        1̶    June 1, 1985 expiration date
     1983    12       15    December 15, 1983 closing date
        1     5       16    unexpired period
```

$370.00 per year   X 1 year   = $370.00
$30.833 per month X 5 months = $154.17
$1.028 per day   X 16 days = $16.45
$370.00 + $154.17 + $16.45 = $540.62

Preparation of deed. The sellers' attorney will prepare their deed, so this agreed expense is debited to the sellers.

Termite inspection. As agreed in the contract, the sellers will pay this expense, so it is debited to them.

Transfer tax. This Illinois transfer tax is $.50 per $500 or fraction thereof of the total purchase price, less the assumed mortgage (the purchase money mortgage is signed by purchasers, so cannot be "assumed" and is considered part of the cash or taxable purchase price).

$123,000 - $52,711.50 assumed mortgage principal = $70,288.50
$70,288.50 ÷ $500 = 140.58 = 141 units of $500
141 X $.50 = $70.50

The transfer tax is charged to the sellers and they are debited with this expense.

Buyers owe. Add all of the buyers' credits. Then, add all of the buyers' debits. In this case, since the debits are greater than the credits, subtract the credits from the debits and the remainder is the amount owed by the buyers.

```
     Total Buyers' Debits      $123,790.62
     Total Buyers' Credits    -  93,598.70
     Buyers Owe                $ 30,191.92
```

Balance due sellers. Add all of the sellers' credits. Then, add all of the sellers' debits. In this case, since the creidts are greater than the debits, subtract the debits from the credits and the remainder is the balance due the sellers.

```
     Total Sellers' Credits    $123,540.62
     Total Sellers' Debits    -  96,132.20
     Balance Due Sellers       $ 27,408.42
```

Now total all four columns at the bottom. The two columns in the buyers' statement should balance, or show the same figure; the two columns in the sellers' statement should also balance with each other. When your worksheet is complete, check all of your entries against the complete settlement worksheet in the Answer Key.

122   ILLINOIS SUPPLEMENT for Modern Real Estate Practice

Recapitulation of Checks and Expenses

This summary is a means of verifying the accuracy of the settlement statement. All cash received by the broker (or in some cases, the attorney) in the transaction is totaled, and the cash disbursed by the broker is subtracted from that total. The resulting balance should be $.00, indicating that there is exactly enough cash to meet all requirements, with no funds left over.

QUESTIONS

1. Which of the following would generally not be credited to the buyer in a four-column closing statement?

    a. earned portion of general real estate taxes
    b. principal of assumed mortgage
    c. transfer tax
    d. earnest money deposit

2. In Illinois, closing statements:

    a. may be prepared by real estate salespeople only under the direct supervision of their brokers.
    b. are generally prepared by escrow agents.
    c. generally involve an expense for the buyer.
    d. all of the above

Compute the following prorations according to the supplied data.

3. Taxes on a property that sold for $79,500 are estimated at $2 per $100 for the full sale price. If the sale is closed on November 1, what is the amount of taxes that will be credited to the buyer at closing?

    a. $265.50
    b. $132.75
    c. $1,327.50
    d. $1,329.42

4. The buyers agree to assume a prepaid two-year fire insurance policy with a total premium of $300. The sale will be closed on July 10, 1982, and the premium for the insurance expires on October 20, 1983. What is the amount that will be credited to the buyers at closing?

    a. $191.53
    b. $191.66
    c. $184.30
    d. none of the above

5. The Nelsons agree to purchase a house for $93,500 subject to their assuming a mortgage with an existing balance of $68,300. What is the amount of transfer tax that must be paid by the sellers at closing?

    a. $53.50
    b. $25.50
    c. $25.00
    d. $47.50

6. When prorating interest on an assumed mortgage loan on which the interest is paid in advance:

    a. the prepaid interest is credited to the buyer.
    b. the unearned interest is credited to the buyer.
    c. the prepaid interest is credited to the seller.
    d. the entire interest is credited to the seller.

7. When property is subject to a special assessment, the annual installment due in the year in which the property is sold is usually:

    a. prorated as to the principal and interest.
    b. paid by the buyer for the entire year.
    c. paid by the seller for the entire year.
    d. paid by the owner of the property when the payment is due on January 2.

8. The entire closing process involves:

    a. computing the prorations expenses, and the amount the buyer owes the seller.
    b. the seller's producing proof of title condition and kind as required by the sales contract.
    c. the buyer paying the seller for his or her deed.
    d. all of the above

9. Complete to make as many true statements as possible: Illinois brokers may

    I. prepare closing statements at the direction of the buyer's and seller's attorneys.
    II. only prepare closing statements that cover the disposition of earnest money and other funds coming into their possession.

    a. I only   c. both I and II
    b. II only   d. neither I nor II

124 ILLINOIS SUPPLEMENT for Modern Real Estate Practice

10. Which of the following acts may a real estate salesperson legally perform in Illinois?

   I. waive the requirement of a written employment agreement between him- or herself and his or her employing broker
   II. withhold from a buyer disclosure of the fact that the owner will accept an offer of less than list price

   a. I only
   b. II only
   c. both I and II
   d. neither I nor II

11. Which of the following statements is NOT true about individuals licensed as real estate salespeople in Illinois?

   a. An active real estate salesperson can be an independent contractor.
   b. An active real estate salesperson must enter into a written employment contract with a real estate broker.
   c. If there is a written employment contract, it must specify the salesperson's compensation and duties.
   d. The written employment can provide for a licensed real estate salesperson to manage a branch office of the brokerage firm.

Answer the following questions based on your completed settlement statement worksheet.

12. The amount of the purchase-money mortgage loan that the sellers are making to the buyers:

   a. is a debit to the buyers.
   b. does not appear on the closing statement.
   c. is $33,389.81.
   d. none of the above

13. The total amount due from the buyers at closing is:

   a. $33,389.81
   b. $27,408.42
   c. $30,191.92
   d. $1,423.00

14. The unpaid balance of the assumed mortgage at closing is:

    a. $53,300.00.
    b. $52,910.00.
    c. $33,389.81.
    d. $52,710.19

15. At the closing the sellers will receive:

    a. $123,540.62.
    b. $7,995.00.
    c. $27,408.42.
    d. $25,934.12.

16. The buyers' total out-of-pocket expenses to be paid at closing are:

    a. $250.00.
    b. $1,423.00.
    c. $1,963.62.
    d. $28,199.04.

Appendix:

The Real Estate License Examination

Modern Real Estate Practice and the Illinois Supplement are designed to prepare you for a career in real estate. But before opening a brokerage office or a salesperson's listing book, you have to obtain a license, for which you must pass an examination--a test of what you've already learned about real estate laws, principles, and practices, and what you know how to do. Each examination reflects the attitudes of the state's real estate licensing agency by stressing the areas of real estate knowledge that its members feel are important.

The Illinois real estate licensing examination is currently prepared and administered by an independent testing service--the Educational Testing Service (ETS). A number of states subscribe to the ETS program. In each state, the program is adapted to local real estate laws and practices and the individual priorities of the state's licensing agency.

WHAT TO EXPECT ON THE EXAM

Salesperson license applicants and broker license applicants will be given different exams. The salesperson's exam, with 130 questions, will be less difficult than the broker's, with 150. Questions will be in the form of multiple-choice problems like the ones at the end of each chapter in this book. Generally, the test will include two types of questions--one to test your knowledge of general real estate and the other to test your ability to solve real estate problems by applying this knowledge.

Questions for both the broker's and salesperson's exams are drawn from the following four major areas:

Real estate law. These deal with the nature of real property, land titles and estates, encumbrances, ownership, acquisition and transfer of real estate, special relationships between persons holding an interest in land, and real estate agents. Questions about real estate law make up approximately 50 percent of the salesperson's exam and about 50 percent of the broker's exam.

Valuation and finance. These deal with the purpose and functions of appraisal, the appraisal process, depreciation, neighborhood analysis, ethics of appraising, mortgage lending agencies, government mortgage institutions, the national economy, the mortgage money market, mathematics of mortgage finance, and truth-in-lending laws. Questions on valuation and finance make up approximately 32 percent of the salesperson's exam and about 25 percent of the broker's exam.

Special fields. These deal with title records, transaction closing, planning and zoning, property management, taxation, subdivisions, mathematics, eminent domain, water rights, economics, urban development, health and safety, and fair housing laws. Questions on these subjects make up approximately 18 percent of the salesperson's exam and about 25 percent of the broker's exam.

Illinois real estate law and other topics. These deal with the Illinois Real Estate License Act, the Illinois Land Registration Act of 1897, consumer protection laws, financing and mortgages, and closing statement theory (broker applicants only). Approximately 23 percent of the questions on the salesperson's exam and about a third of the ones on the broker's exam are about Illinois topics.

The questions from the first three topic areas are of a general nature, while the questions developed for the fourth topic group pertain specifically to Illinois laws, principles, and practices. The Illinois questions were written by real estate instructors and practitioners throughout the state under the supervision of ETS. As you might imagine, some topic areas, such as real estate finance, are represented by both general questions and questions specific to Illinois. In either case, you will not be expected to answer any questions about topics of specific details that do not apply to Illinois laws and practices or that do not appear on the state-approved course outline from which your real estate instructor is required to teach.

Salesperson's Examination

The Illinois real estate salesperson's exam consists of 130 multiple-choice questions. The exam lasts approximately three and one-half hours. Unlike the broker's exam, it does not include questions based on closing statement prorations and computations. However, salesperson applicants are expected to complete basic problems in real estate mathematics related to such topics as commissions, interest, and area and volume.

Note that only silent, cordless electronic calculators that do not have a permanent memory are permitted in the testing center at the time of the exam.

Sample questions. The questions on the exam are not set up to trick you. You will, however, encounter several exam questions that are more complex than the rest. Such questions are usually in a story format. Read each question carefully to know exactly what is being asked before you begin to formulate your answer. Questions most difficult for examinees include those with superfluous facts, synthesis of facts, reading comprehension, multi-step math, value judgments, best answer, and "super" multiple-choice.

Exam questions frequently contain superfluous facts that are not needed to answer the question. For example:

Appendix: The Real Estate License Examination   129

> The Koepkes paid $50,000 for their home five years ago, making a $10,000 down payment. Their monthly payments, including interest at 7-3/4 percent, amounted to $286. The interest portion of their last payment was $225.27. What was their approximate loan balance before their last payment?

The only facts you need to answer this question are the amount of the last interest payment and the rate of interest. To solve you simply multiply the amount of the monthly interest, $225.27, by 12. You then divide the result by the interest rate, .0775, to get the approximate loan balance ($34,880.52).

Another type of question asks you to take facts that you have learned separately and <u>synthesize</u> that information to answer the question. For example:

> Twelve years ago the Paul Zieglers, parents of two children, retired and left Berwyn, Illinois, taking up residence in Alabama along the Gulf Coast. They decided to keep their Berwyn residence, which they owned as tenants in common, renting it to friends. Mae Ziegler died suddenly leaving no will. Alabama law provides that when a wife dies intestate, a widower receives a life estate in all real property owned by his wife at death. Paul's interest in the Berwyn home is:
>
>   a. in severalty due to the right of survivorship.
>   b. a life estate.
>   c. one-half interest.
>   d. three-fourths interest.

The correct answer is d. To answer this question you need to know: (1) that rights of survivorship do not apply to a tenancy in common; (2) that Illinois property is probated in Illinois in accordance with Illinois law; (3) that the laws of descent apply because the wife died intestate; (4) what the laws of descent are in Illinois; and (5) how to combine numerically the real estate interests held before and after the wife's death.

The third type of question you may find on the test requires you to read each word extremely carefully for <u>comprehension</u>. For example:

> Closing of a transaction for a residential property is set for April 19, 1983. Seller has a three-year insurance policy that expires June 25, 1984. Seller has prepaid a three-year premium of $762. Buyer is to take over the policy as of the date of closing. The amount credited to the buyer at closing is:
>
>   a. $254.00.
>   b. $300.57.
>   c. $461.57.
>   d. none of the above

The answer here is d because the prorated amount of the prepaid insurance would be debited to the buyer.

Another type of question that frequently appears is the <u>multi-step math</u> question. For example:

> Karen Valentine bought a house at exactly the appraised value. She negotiated a loan through Prairieville Savings and Loan Association at 75 percent of the appraised value. The interest rate was 9 percent. The first month's interest was $405. What was the selling price of the property?

To answer this question, you must first multiply $405 by 12 to get the annual interest ($4,860). You then divide $4,860 by the interest rate, .09, to get the amount of the loan ($54,000). Next you divide $54,000 by .75 to find the appraised value ($72,000), which is the same as the purchase price.

A few questions on the exam may ask you to make a value judgment. For example:

> Broker Howard Smedloe listed a small house owned by George Miller at $26,000, obtaining an executed sales contract on it within six weeks at $25,000. Smedloe learned there was an existing $15,000 first mortgage and a $5,000 second mortgage on the property. Smedloe knew the real estate could be refinanced on a new $20,000 first mortgage loan. The holder of the second mortgage, Peter Frye, told Smedloe he was willing to discount his $5,000 note, selling it for $4,500. The buyer has $5,000 cash and qualifies for a new $20,000 first mortgage loan. Smedloe should:
>
> a. say nothing to Miller about refinancing and allow the transaction to close.
> b. tell Miller the second mortgage can be paid off at a $500 discount.
> c. tell Frye the property is sold and therefore he should demand the full amount of $5,000.
> d. buy the second mortgage himself at the $500 discount.

The answer, of course, is b. As an agent of the seller, the broker must act in the seller's best interest. Furthermore, alternative d would be illegal, as the broker would become a principal in the transaction without informing anyone.

You will frequently be asked to choose the best answer from alternatives when the ideal answer is not present. For example:

> Broker Harmon Lowrie listed Louise Navarro's beachfront home at $78,000. Three weeks later Lowrie obtained a full-price offer on the beach house from Scott Lasser. Stopping by the house after the sales contract was executed and in force, Lowrie was appalled to see a large foundation crack. Two days later Lowrie noticed that the crack had been carefully repaired. Lowrie knew that seller Navarro was unaware of the crack because she was over 80 with extremely poor eyesight. Lowrie suspected the crack was fixed by Ms. Navarro's son-in-law, a building contractor. Lowrie should:
>
> a. disclose the fact of the crack to buyer Lasser.
> b. immediately cancel the sales contract.
> c. keep quiet about the crack since it has been repaired.
> d. confront the son-in-law with his suspicions and threaten to sue.

The best alternative available here is a. The better answer, "inform seller Navarro of the crack, requesting permission to inform buyer Lasser," does not appear here. Note that this question also asks you to make a value judgment.

Finally, you may find some questions in the "super" multiple-choice format. For example:

> Shirley Kominsky is the manager of a 25-unit apartment building in Oak Park. To attract tenants for the building she may legally:
>
> I. have brochures printed and distribute them to the public.
> II. place display ads in the Oak Park paper.
>
>   a. I only   c. both I and II
>   b. II only   d. neither I nor II

The answer here, of course, is c. Property managers may use both of the above means to advertise their apartments.

Broker's Examination

The Illinois real estate broker's exam consists of 150 multiple-choice questions designed to test the applicant in greater detail than the ones in the salesperson's exam. The broker's exam lasts approximately four and one-half hours, and includes several questions based on a settlement statement worksheet (closing statement) that the applicant is asked to complete.

Chapter 23 of the Illinois Supplement includes a closing problem based on a case history (story) of a typical residential real estate transaction. The case history, the settlement statement worksheet and instructions on how to complete it, and the questions at the end of the chapter are similar to what you will find on the examination. In computing prorations for these problems, you will be asked to base your computations on a particular method specified in the problem which may not necessarily be the method you are accustomed to using. For example, a question may instruct you to compute a proration problem based on the actual number of days in the month of closing, with all calculations carried out to two decimal places. It is important to follow exactly the directions given in the problem.

Preparing for the License Examination

We have tried to prepare you for the Illinois real estate licensing examination by including in the Illinois Supplement the kinds of items usually found on the test. Your most important preparation for the test involves studying real estate principles, practices and laws. Concentrate on learning the material by studying both Modern Real Estate Practice and the Illinois Supplement and by working all the tests and exercises, paying particularly close attention to those problems you may have originally missed. Remember, you will be asked to apply your knowledge to situations, combining facts and principles as illustrated in this Appendix.

132   ILLINOIS SUPPLEMENT for Modern Real Estate Practice

TAKING THE LICENSE EXAMINATION

For best results, start by going through the entire examination, answering those questions you are certain about. By leaving the doubtful ones for last, you make sure you have time to mark all the answers you know are correct. Once you've answered all the questions you feel sure about, return to the remaining questions. If you are unable to arrive at an answer the second time through, guess. There is no penalty for guessing. The answers to the examination are marked mechanically, so be careful to mark only the chosen answer block.

Your state of mind as you take the examination can be almost as important as your knowledge of the material. Try to relax--loosen up any tension you feel. This will allow your mind to work at high efficiency and make good use of all the knowledge you have gained through study and practice. If you apply your preparation and study to the test, there is no reason you won't pass it.

SAMPLE FINAL EXAMINATION

1. The Poores paid 4 1/2 points as a loan origination fee to Richland Savings and Loan when they obtained their mortgage loan. Richland immediately sold the loan at a 4 percent discount, receiving $78,720. What was the original amount of the Poores' loan?

    a. $86,000
    b. $75,571
    c. $82,000
    d. $82,430

2. Tess Scarz, a sales associate with Apple Realty, listed and sold Charlie Booker's vacant lot in a residential area. The 90 foot wide by 150 foot deep lot sold for $185 a front foot. If Apple received a 10 percent brokerage fee on the vacant property and paid the listing salesperson 35 percent and the selling salesperson 25 percent of the commission, what did Tess receive in this transaction?

    a. $582.75
    b. $999.00
    c. $416.25
    d. $1,665.00

3. Vitalis is a squatter who has been in continuous, illegal, notorious, unauthorized possession of Mericle's five-acre field for 19 years. Mericle passes the lot and finds it overgrown with noxious weeds and orders the weeds to be cut. The cutting machine ceases to function when it contacts Vitalis asleep in his nest. In order that Vitalis will acquire no rights to cloud Mericle's fee simple title, she must have Vitalis evicted before his occupancy totals:

   a. 7 years.
   b. 13 years.
   c. 20 years.
   d. 21 years.

4. Jack Holden devised all of his real estate to his son Junior. After Jack's death Junior will hold:

   a. a fee simple estate.
   b. a life estate.
   c. an estate in remainder.
   d. whatever estate Jack owned.

5. George Sonner borrowed $50,000 from a private lender, using the services of Turner Mortgage and Loan Company. He received $47,000 after the loan costs and broker's commission. The face amount of the note was:

   a. $47,000.
   b. $50,000.
   c. $62,500.
   d. none of the above

6. Which of the following statements is true?

   a. In Illinois, a deed must be acknowledged before it is recorded or registered.
   b. Everything that is not real estate is considered personal property.
   c. Under Illinois law, a judgment lien is a specific lien.
   d. Ownership in severalty refers to joint ownership of real property.

7. Fred Marshall transferred the title to a parcel of commercial property to his son John for life. John then leased the property to Bob Stones to use as a laundry. After John is killed in a sailing accident, Bob Stones holds:

   a. a reversionary interest.
   b. a life estate.
   c. a tenancy at sufferance.
   d. a tenancy at will.

8. Sheedy sold his bee farm to Herman. Title to the property was conveyed when:

   a. Herman had the deed recorded.
   b. the deed was acknowledged.
   c. the deed was executed.
   d. Sheedy delivered the deed to Herman.

9. Illinois law states that all contracts for sale of land and all leases for longer than one year must be in writing to be enforceable. This law or rule is known as:

   a. the statute of frauds.
   b. the statute of limitations.
   c. the Professional Ethics Code.
   d. none of the above

10. A subordination involves:

    a. only a first mortgage.
    b. a recorded quitclaim deed.
    c. the priority of two liens.
    d. the dominant tenement of an easement appurtenant.

11. A parcel of commercial property sold for $78,000 at a foreclosure sale of the first mortgage of $91,000 held by Majority Savings and Loan. Shirley Schwartz held a second mortgage of $7,000. What will Schwartz receive from the proceeds of the sale?

    a. $7,000
    b. $6,000
    c. $4,500
    d. nothing

12. A valid restriction on the use of real property may also be called:

    a. a lien.
    b. an encumbrance.
    c. an easement by prescription.
    d. a cloud on the title.

13. The McMasters have a rectangular lot that contains 9,625 square feet. The lot is 175 feet deep. They want to put a privacy fence across the back of the lot. Materials and labor for the fence cost $10.80 a running foot. How much will the fence cost?

    a. $1,890.00
    b. $1,750.00
    c. $1,039.50
    d. $594.00

14. Section 6 is always in the:

    a. southeast corner of a township.
    b. southwest corner of a township.
    c. northeast corner of a township.
    d. northwest corner of a township.

15. Hill and Dale Realty listed a lovely five-bedroom house at $130,000. The home sold for 12 percent less than the list price. Hill and Dale charged 6 1/2 percent commission on the first $100,000 and 6 percent for the excess above $100,000. What was the seller's net after commission?

    a. $121,700
    b. $108,400
    c. $107,900
    d. $107,036

16. Sandra Chandler of Miami wants to sell lots in her new subdivision, Surfside Acres, Florida, to Illinois residents. With which of the following Illinois laws must Chandler comply?

    a. Illinois Subdivision Plat Act
    b. Illinois Real Estate License Act
    c. Illinois Land Sales Act
    d. all of the above

17. George and Paulette Lincoln have just sold their home on which they had an FHA-insured loan. By federal law, the prepayment penalty that they can be charged may not exceed:

    a. two percent of the remaining balance at the time of the prepayment.
    b. 120 days' interest on the current loan balance.
    c. one percent of the original loan amount.
    d. zero

18. After deducting 6 1/2 percent commission and selling expenses of $137, the Harrells received $77,000.50 for the sale of their home. The gross price was:

    a. $82,353.
    b. $82,490.
    c. $82,500.
    d. $85,000.

19. Which of the following would not be considered real property?

    a. coal that is not yet mined
    b. display cases that have been bolted down in a leased retail store
    c. garages in the rear of an apartment building
    d. fences around a condominium complex

20. The term "lessee" is generally used to describe:

    a. a tenant.
    b. a vendee.
    c. an optionee.
    d. an owner.

21. Candy Johnson acquired a house in Peoria under the terms of her uncle's will. Candy is:

    a. a devisee.
    b. an executrix.
    c. a decedent.
    d. an administratrix.

22. Mooney, who owns a duplex apartment building in Ottawa, Illinois, orally agreed with Higgins upon a nine-month lease of one of Mooney's units at a monthly rental of $475. Before he moved in, Higgins changed his mind, claiming it was not a valid lease. Which of the following statements is true?

    a. The lease is invalid because it is not in writing.
    b. The lease is valid.
    c. The lease is invalid because Mooney did not collect the first month's rent.
    d. The lease does not comply with the statute of frauds.

23. An acceleration clause in a mortgage note principally benefits the:

    a. lender.
    b. borrower.
    c. broker.
    d. trustee.

24. Which of the following contains the smallest area?

    a. 4 sections
    b. 4 miles square
    c. 1/4 of a township
    d. 5,280 feet x 26,400 feet

25. Harold Hill in 1973 purchased the NE 1/4 of the NE 1/4 of section 5 and the N 1/2 of the NW 1/4 of section 4, paying $4,000 an acre. He got an 80 percent loan on which the outstanding balance is now 24 percent of the face value of the original note. What is the present loan balance?

    a. $115,200
    b. $92,160
    c. $38,400
    d. $61,440

26. Martha and John Utley listed their home at $75,000. It was finally sold, netting the Utleys $66,665. They paid 6 1/2 percent commission and closing expenses of $187.50. What was the selling price?

   a. $75,000
   b. $71,500
   c. $71,300
   d. $70,500

27. Irma Martin, a salesperson, has a property she would like to picture in a display ad. Her broker does not want to pay for a display ad on the property at this time. Martin may advertise the property herself only if:

   a. she pays for the ad entirely out of past commissions.
   b. she personally listed the property.
   c. she includes her broker's name in the ad.
   d. all of the above

28. Pat Keogh assigned her apartment lease to Tim McMahon. Which statement is true?

   a. Tim is now subleasing from Pat.
   b. Pat has retained the right to use the apartment for a period of time.
   c. The entire leasehold interest has been transferred to Tim.
   d. none of the above

29. Fred Lounger decided to divide two acres of land into ten equal sized lots, 135 feet deep. What is the approximate front footage of each lot?

   a. 32 feet
   b. 55 feet
   c. 65 feet
   d. 75 feet

30. The principal east and west line used in a description by the Rectangular Survey System is called the:

   a. township line.
   b. range line.
   c. base line.
   d. Principal Meridian.

31. Professor Karen Wilkins listed her house for $75,000. It sold four weeks later for $70,400. She had made a 10 percent profit in 14 months. What was the amount of her profit?

   a. $7,744
   b. $7,622
   c. $7,040
   d. $6,400

32. The right of survivorship always exists in a:

    a. tenancy in common.
    b. condominium.
    c. joint tenancy.
    d. cooperative.

33. A section:

    a. contains one square mile.
    b. measures 320 rods on each side.
    c. equals 5,280 feet by 5,280 feet.
    d. all of the above

34. The Michaelsons sold their home to Willard Morris. Through an agreement with the Local Savings and Loan, Morris was able to assume the Michaelsons' loan. Which of the following statements is true?

    a. The Michaelsons are entirely relieved of their responsibility to repay the loan.
    b. The Michaelsons remain solely responsible to pay off the note.
    c. If Morris stops making payments on the loan, Morris can be held liable.
    d. If Local Savings and Loan forecloses, Morris can lose the property but cannot be sued for a deficiency judgment.

35. O'Malley Materials was a subcontractor on a remodeling job done for Joseph Stahl. Although Stahl paid Honor Construction, the general contractor, O'Malley never collected. Which of the following statements is true?

    a. O'Malley can file a subordination lien on Stahl's property where the work was done.
    b. O'Malley can file a judgment lien against Stahl.
    c. O'Malley can file an attachment lien against Honor Construction.
    d. O'Malley can file a mechanic's lien on the house that was remodeled for Stahl.

36. Stan Healy, a life-long Illinois resident, died intestate leaving no heirs that could be traced. His property will:

    a. escheat to the state.
    b. escheat to the county.
    c. escheat equally to the county and state.
    d. be placed in a special probate fund.

37. The Leakes bought the Thornes's home in Libertyville. Closing was set for December 12, 1983. The Thornes have paid $836.51 for the first installment and a $932.67 second installment on 1982 real estate taxes. The amount debited to the Thornes at closing for real estate taxes would be:

    a. $1,474.31.
    b. $1,621.74.
    c. $1.680.71.
    d. $1,769.80.

38. Cookie Lutz is broker Irving Swartz's secretary. She does not hold an Illinois real estate salesperson's license. Which of the following statements is true?

    a. It is legal for Cookie to lease apartments in properties that Swartz manages.
    b. Cookie may legally give callers information regarding the listed price of properties.
    c. Swartz may legally require Cookie to make calls to prospective sellers soliciting listings when she has spare time.
    d. none of the above

39. Leonard Pierogi told his banker he needed a blanket mortgage loan. He meant that he needed a loan that:

    a. would consolidate several small mortgage loans.
    b. covered both real and personal property.
    c. would cover more than one piece of property.
    d. would allow him to renegotiate after five years to get a larger loan.

40. The words "time is of the essence" generally appear in a:

    a. lease.
    b. sales contract.
    c. listing contract.
    d. mortgage.

41. Jack Dunne is having one of his commercial properties appraised. The most important of the following factors for the appraiser to consider is the:

    a. cost of reproduction.
    b. depreciation.
    c. gross income.
    d. net income.

42. Sarah Farmer bought a condominium unit from Ted Hightower, agreeing also to buy his living room furniture. To ensure that she gets title to the furniture, Sarah should request from Ted a:

    a. chattel deed.
    b. contract for sale.
    c. bill of sale.
    d. vendor's acknowledgment.

43. The beams to which floors and ceiling are attached are called:

    a. rafters.
    b. studs.
    c. joists.
    d. footings.

44. Nate Hawkinson wanted to find a 25- to 30-unit apartment building and make an offer to purchase based on a gross rent multiplier of 8 1/2 times the gross annual rents. He soon found a 24-unit building he liked so well he decided to make an offer. Twelve of the apartments rented for $370 per month, another eight rented for $450, and the four penthouses rented for $630. Hawkinson's offer should amount to:

    a. $897,600.
    b. $1,013,760.
    c. $1,077,120.
    d. $1,140,480.

45. Broker Ron Reitzel has an agreement with Stuart Lee that gives him a right to collect a commission no matter who sells Lee's property. Reitzel has an:

    a. exclusive agency listing.
    b. open listing.
    c. exclusive-right-to-sell listing.
    d. option.

46. The Cattlemans want to buy the Barnes's home but must first sell their present home. What is the appropriate clause to insert in the sales contract to cover this?

    a. subordination clause
    b. alienation clause
    c. contingency clause
    d. substitution clause

47. Marc Downes is an inexperienced appraiser. He decided to use the cost approach to appraise a residence built around the turn of the century. This is an inefficient method because of:

   a. estimating depreciation.
   b. changes in building codes.
   c. changes in costs of materials.
   d. changes in labor rates.

48. Peg Huber set up a testamentary trust so that her daughter Jill would receive the benefit of all her real property. Jill is known as the:

   a. trustee.
   b. trustor.
   c. testator.
   d. none of the above

49. Joel Smikler was forced to sell part of the land in front of his house because of the widening of the state highway on which he lives. This is an example of:

   a. a zoning variation.
   b. police power.
   c. escheat.
   d. eminent domain.

50. When Tom French purchased his new home, the deed was recorded in the Cook County recorder's office. Who may see these records?

   a. Tom and his wife
   b. Tom's neighbors whom he doesn't like
   c. tax assessor
   d. all of the above

51. Carol Irey signed a listing agreement on her residence with broker Mary Ann Fieri. This contract may be terminated if:

   I. Irey or Fieri dies during the listing period.
   II. the building burns down.

   a. I only   c. both I and II
   b. II only   d. neither I nor II

52. Moody sold her house to Dietrich, who agreed to pay a specified amount on a monthly basis. The records show Moody is still owner. Which of the following may be true?

   I. Dietrich is buying the house on contract.
   II. The property is now in a recorded trust.

   a. I only
   b. II only
   c. both I and II
   d. neither I nor II

53. To hold property in joint tenancy in Illinois, persons must:

   I. be husband and wife.
   II. agree that the survivor gets deceased's share.

   a. I only
   b. II only
   c. both I and II
   d. neither I nor II

54. Cora Scott decided to subdivide her 15 acres into quarter-acre lots and sell them. Cora must first:

   I. comply with the terms of the Illinois Plat Act.
   II. obtain a real estate securities license.

   a. I only
   b. II only
   c. both I and II
   d. neither I nor II

55. Which of the following interests in real estate may be termed "less than a freehold estate"?

   I. an estate for years
   II. a leasehold estate

   a. I only
   b. II only
   c. both I and II
   d. neither I nor II

56. Shallot, a qualified buyer, made a written offer to buy Marconi's residence at $3,000 less than the list price through the listing broker, Bean. Marconi accepted the offer in writing and Bean notified Shallot. Three days later the son of one of Marconi's neighbors gave him a full-price offer. So, Marconi told Bean he was no longer interested in selling to Shallot. Which of the following is true?

    a. Bean has no claim for a commission from Marconi.
    b. Bean can void the contract with Shallot and claim a commission on the full-price offer.
    c. Bean has a valid claim for a commission on the Shallot contract.
    d. Bean can claim half of the commission on the Shallot offer.

57. John and Joan own their home in tenancy by entirety. Sarah and Sam her husband buy an investment property as joint tenants. Peter, Paul, and Mary buy an apartment and take title as joint tenants. What do the preceding owners have in common?

    a. They all have a leasehold interest in their properties.
    b. They all have a right of survivorship.
    c. They all acquire title that will pass to their heirs.
    d. They all must get approval from their partner(s) before they sell their interests.

58. Johannah, an Illinois resident, died without leaving a will. Which of the following statements is or are <u>not</u> true?

    I. She has died intestate.
    II. Her estate automatically escheats to the county.

    a. I only   c. both I and II
    b. II only   d. neither I nor II

59. Which of the following is (are) considered an encumbrance on real estate?

    I. a mortgage
    II. an easement

    a. I only   c. both I and II
    b. II only   d. neither I nor II

Answer Key

In the answers following, the numbers in parentheses refer to page numbers where the topic begins -- S means a page in this supplement, T means a page in Modern Real Estate Practice.

Chapter 5
1. B (S2)
2. B (S1)
3. D (S2)
4. B (S1)
5. C (T53)
6. C (S2,3)
7. C (S3)
8. A (S1)

Chapter 6
1. A (S1)
2. D (S7)
3. D (S7)
4. C (T69)
5. B (S7)
6. D (T72)

Chapter 7
1. B (S12)
2. A (S12)
3. D (S11)
4. C (S11)
5. C (S12)
6. B (T91)
7. D (T85)
8. A (T85)
9. C (T91)

Chapter 8
1. A (S15)
2. D (S16)
3. A (S15)
4. A (S16)
5. D (S18)
6. A (S16)
7. B (S15)
8. C (T108)
9. A (S18)
10. B (S18)
11. B (S16)
12. B (S15)
13. C (S15)
14. D (S15)

Chapter 9
1. A (S23)
2. D (S26)
3. C (S26)
4. A (T127)
5. C (S20)
6. C (S19)
7. D (S19)
8. B (T127)
9. D (T127)
10. C
11. C
12. C
13. C
14. B

Chapter 10
1. B (S31)
2. A (S35)
3. A (S35)
4. D (S34)
5. A (S33)
6. D (S32)
7. D (S35)
8. C (S35)
9. D (T136)
10. B (T136)
11. A (S32)

Chapter 11
1. D (S40)
2. A (S39)
3. D (S40)
4. D (S39)
5. C (T151)
6. C (S39)
7. D (S41)
8. C (S40)
9. C (S39)
10. B (T160)
11. C (T153)
12. D (S41)

Chapter 12
1. B (S45)
2. D (S46)
3. A (S47)
4. B (S48)
5. D (S48)
6. C (S45)
7. B (S48)
8. C (S45)
9. D (S45)
10. C (S45)
11. D (T102)
12. A (S48)
13. A (S48)
14. B (S48)
15. D (S48)
16. D

Chapter 13
1. D (S59)
2. A (S60)
3. D (S59)
4. C (S59)
5. D (S59)
6. C (S61)
7. B (S60)
8. A (T192)
9. C (S60)
10. A (S60)

Chapter 14
1. A (S73)
2. D (S71)
3. B (S69)
4. A (S81)
5. B (S83)
6. B (S81)
7. B (S81)
8. C (S72)
9. C (S70)
10. C (S72)
11. D (S73)
12. D (S81)
13. D (S73)
14. B (S70)
15. B (S66)
16. D (S77)
17. B (S69)
18. B (S79)
19. D (S66)
20. C (S80)
21. A (S72)
22. A (S73)

Chapter 15
1. C (S91)
2. C (S92)
3. D (S92)
4. C (S92)
5. B (S92)
6. A (S91)
7. D (T242)
8. B (T220)
9. C (T221)

Chapter 16
1. A (S97)
2. C (S98)
3. A (S98)
4. C (S98)
5. B (S99)
6. D (S97)
7. B (S98)
8. D (S99)
9. B (S98)

Chapters 19/20
1. A (S103)
2. C (S103)
3. C (S103)

Chapter 21
1. C (S107)
2. A (S107)
3. B (S107)
4. C (S107)
5. D (S107)
6. A (S107)
7. C (S107)

Chapter 23
1. C (S121)
2. A (S113)
3. D (S120)
4. D (S121)
5. B (S121)
6. C (S114)
7. D (S114)
8. D (S113)
9. A (S113)
10. B (S2)
11. D (S76)
12. C
13. C
14. D
15. C
16. A

Final Exam

1. C	16. C	31. D	46. C
2. B	17. D	32. C	47. A
3. C	18. C	33. D	48. D
4. D	19. B	34. C	49. D
5. B	20. A	35. D	50. D
6. B	21. A	36. B	51. C
7. C	22. B	37. C	52. A
8. D	23. A	38. D	53. B
9. A	24. A	39. C	54. A
10. C	25. B	40. B	55. C
11. D	26. B	41. D	56. C
12. B	27. C	42. C	57. B
13. D	28. C	43. C	58. A
14. D	29. C	44. C	59. C
15. D	30. C	45. C	

SETTLEMENT STATEMENT WORKSHEET

Property: 811 Stowell Drive, Palatine, Illinois 60067 - Cook Cty.
Seller: Ryan and Erin Bowman
Buyer: Brian and Toni Morrow
Settlement Date: Dec. 15, 1983

	BUYER'S STATEMENT		SELLER'S STATEMENT	
	DEBIT	CREDIT	DEBIT	CREDIT
Purchase Price	123,000.00			123,000.00
Earnest Money Deposit		6,150.00		
Assumed Mortgage Principal		52,710.19	52,710.19	
Prorated Mortgage Interest		175.70	175.70	
Purchase Money Mortgage		33,389.81	33,389.81	
Real Estate Tax		1,173.00	1,173.00	
Broker's Commission			7,995.00	
Preparation of Purch. Money Mort.	100.00			
Recording Fees	20.00			
Settlement Charge	50.00			
Title Insurance	80.00		468.00	
Fire & Hazard Insurance - Prorated	540.62			540.62
Preparation of Deed			100.00	
Termite Inspection			50.00	
Transfer Tax			70.50	
Total Debits & Credits	123,790.62	93,598.70	96,132.20	123,540.62
Due from Buyer at Close		30,191.92		
Due Seller at Close			27,408.42	
	123,790.62	123,790.62	123,540.62	123,540.62

Real Estate License Act of 1983

Public Act 83-191, effective January 1, 1984

AN ACT to revise the law in relation to the definition, registration and regulation of real estate brokers, real estate associate brokers and real estate salespersons, and to amend or repeal certain Acts herein named.

SECTION 1. The intent of the General Assembly in enacting this statute is to evaluate the competency of persons engaged in the real estate business and to regulate such business for the protection of the public.

SECTION 2. This Act shall be known and may be cited as the Real Estate License Act of 1983, and it shall supersede the Real Estate Brokers and Salesmen License Act repealed by this Act.

SECTION 3. It is unlawful for any person to act as a real estate broker, associate real estate broker or real estate salesperson, or to advertise or assume to act as such broker, associate broker or salesperson, without a license issued by the Department of Registration and Education. No partnership or corporation shall be granted a license, or engage in the business or capacity, either directly or indirectly, of a real estate broker, unless every partner in such partnership or every officer of such corporation who actively participates in the brokerage business of such partnership or corporation holds a license as a real estate broker, and unless every employee who acts as a salesperson for such partnership or corporation holds a license as a real estate salesperson. Nothing in this Act shall prohibit the cooperation of, or a division of commissions between, a duly licensed broker of this State and a nonresident broker having no office in this State.

SECTION 4. As used in this Act, unless the context otherwise requires:

(1) "Applicant" means any person, as defined in subsection (14) of this Section, who applies to the Department for a valid license as a real estate broker, real estate associate broker, or real estate salesperson.

(2) "Associate Broker" means an individual who has a real estate broker's license and who is employed by another real estate broker, or is associated with another real estate broker as an independent contractor, or is associated by written agreement with another real estate broker and participates in any activity described in subsection (5) of this Section.

(3) "Board" means the Real Estate Administration and Disciplinary Board of the Department.

(4) "Branch Office" means a real estate broker's office other than the broker's principal place of business.

(5) "Broker" means an individual other than a real estate salesperson, partnership or corporation, who for another and for compensation:

(a) Sells, exchanges, purchases, rents, or leases real estate.

(b) Offers to sell, exchange, purchase, rent or lease real estate.

(c) Negotiates, offers, attempts or agrees to negotiate the sale, exchange, purchase, rental or leasing of real estate.

(d) Lists, offers, attempts or agrees to list real estate for sale, lease or exchange.

(e) Buys, sells, offers to buy or sell or otherwise deals in options on real estate or improvements thereon.

(f) Collects, offers, attempts or agrees to collect rent for the use of real estate.

(g) Advertises or represents himself as being engaged in the business of buying, selling, exchanging, renting or leasing real estate.

(h) Assists or directs in procuring of prospects, intended to result in the sale, exchange, lease or rental of real estate.

(i) Assists or directs in the negotiation of any transaction intended to result in the sale, exchange, leasing or rental of real estate.

(6) "Commissioner" means the Commissioner of Real Estate of the Department.

(7) "Department" means the Department of Registration and Education.

(8) "Director" means the Director of the Department.

(9) "Employee" or other derivative of the word "employee" when used to refer to, describe or delineate the relationship between a real estate broker and a real estate salesperson or real estate associate broker shall be construed to include an independent contractor relationship provided that there exists a written agreement clearly establishing and stating such a relationship. All responsibilities of a broker shall remain.

(10) "Financial Institution" means a bank or savings and loan institution or credit union chartered by the federal government or any state of the United States.

(11) "License" means the document issued by the Department certifying that the person named thereon has fulfilled all requirements prerequisite to registration under this Act. License includes the term "certificate".

(12) "Licensee" means any person, as defined in subsection (14) of this Section, who holds a valid license as a real estate broker, real estate associate broker or real estate salesperson.

(13) "Office" means a real estate broker's place of business located within a structure used either for residential or commercial purposes, where records may be maintained and licenses displayed, whether or not it is the broker's principal place of business.

(14) "Person" means and includes individuals, corporations and partnerships, foreign or domestic, except that when referring to a person licensed under this Act it may mean only an individual.

(15) "Real Estate" means and includes leaseholds, as well as any other interest or estate in land, whether corporeal, incorporeal, freehold or non-freehold, and whether the real estate is situated in this State or elsewhere.

(16) "Real Estate School" means a school approved by the Department offering work in subjects related to real estate transactions; including the subjects upon which an applicant is examined in determining fitness to receive a license.

(17) "Registration Pocket Card" means the card issued by the Department to signify that the person named on such card is currently licensed under this Act.

(18) "Salesperson" means any individual, other than a real estate broker or associate broker, who is employed by a real estate broker or is associated by written agreement with a real estate broker as an independent contractor and participates in any activity described in subsection (5) of this Section.

(19) "Sponsor Card" means the card issued by a real estate broker certifying that the real estate broker, real

ILLINOIS REAL ESTATE LICENSE ACT

estate associate broker or real estate salesperson named thereon is employed by or associated by written agreement with such real estate broker.

SECTION 5. The commission of a single act prohibited by this Act constitutes a violation of this Act.

SECTION 6. The provisions of this Act shall not apply to:

(1) Any person, partnership or corporation who as owner or lessor shall perform any of the acts described in subsection (5) of Section 4 of this Act with reference to property owned or leased by them, or to the regular employees thereof with respect to the property so owned or leased, where such acts are performed in the regular course of or as an incident to the management, sale or other disposition of such property and the investment therein, provided that such regular employees shall not perform any of the acts described is subsection (5) of Section 4 of this Act in connection with a vocation of selling or leasing any real estate or the improvements thereon not so owned or leased.

(2) An attorney in fact acting under a duly executed and recorded power of attorney to convey real estate from the owner or lessor, or the services rendered by an attorney at law in the performance of the attorney's duty as such attorney at law.

(3) Any person acting as receiver, trustee in bankruptcy, administrator, executor or guardian or while acting under a court order or under the authority of a will or of a trust instrument.

(4) Any person acting as a resident manager for the owner or any employee acting as the resident manager for a broker managing an apartment building, duplex, apartment complex or court, when such resident manager resides on the premises and is engaged in the leasing of property in connection with such employment.

(5) Any officer or employee of a federal agency in the conduct of his official duties.

(6) Any officer or employee of the State government or any political subdivision thereof performing his official duties.

(7) Any multiple listing service wholly owned by a not-for-profit organization or association of real estate brokers.

(8) Any not-for-profit referral system or organization of real estate brokers formed for the purpose of referrals of prospects for the sale or listing of real estate.

(9) Railroads and other public utilities regulated by the State of Illinois, or their subsidiaries or affiliated corporations, or to the officers or regular employees thereof, unless performance of any of the acts described in subsection (5) of Section 4 of this Act is in connection with the sale, purchase, lease or other disposition of real estate or investment therein unrelated to the regulated business activity of such railroad or other public utility or affiliated or subsidiary corporation thereof.

SECTION 7. No action or suit shall be instituted, nor recovery therein be had, in any court of this State by any person, partnership or corporation for compensation for any act done or service performed, the doing or performing of which is prohibited by this Act to other than licensed brokers, associate brokers or salespersons unless such person, partnership or corporation was duly licensed hereunder as a broker or salesperson prior to the time of offering to perform any such act or service or procuring any promise or contract for the payment of compensation for any such contemplated act or service.

SECTION 8. The Department shall exercise the powers and duties prescribed by The Civil Administrative Code of Illinois for the administration of licensing acts, and shall exercise such other powers and duties as are prescribed by this Act.

SECTION 9. There is created the Real Estate Administration and Disciplinary Board, hereinafter referred to as the "Board". The Board shall be composed of 7 persons, who have been residents and citizens of this State for at least 6 years prior to the date of appointment, 5 of whom have been actively engaged as a broker or salesperson or both for at least the 10 years prior to such appointment and are not affiliated, either directly or indirectly, with any school regulated by the Department pursuant to this Act, and 2 of whom shall be representative of the public at large. The members' terms shall be 4 years, but no more than 2 members' terms shall expire in any one year. Appointments to fill vacancies shall be for the unexpired portion of the term.

A member may be reappointed for successive terms but no member shall serve more than 10 years in his lifetime. (Service prior to the effective date of this Act shall not be considered.)

Persons holding office as members of the Examining Committee immediately prior to the effective date of this Act under the Act repealed herein shall continue as members of the Board until the expiration of the term for which they were appointed and until their successors are appointed and qualified.

The membership of the Board should reasonably reflect representation from the geographic areas in this State. In making such appointments, the Director shall give due consideration to the recommendations by members and organizations of the profession.

The Director may terminate the appointment of any member for cause which in the opinion of the Director reasonably justifies such termination.

Each member of the Board shall receive a per-diem stipend as the Director shall determine. Each member shall be paid his necessary expenses while engaged in the performance of his duties. Such compensation and expenses shall be paid out of the Real Estate License Administration Fund.

The Director shall consider the recommendations of the Board on questions involving standards of professional conduct, discipline and examination of candidates under this Act.

The Director, on the recommendation of the Board, may issue rules, consistent with the provisions of this Act, for the administration and enforcement thereof and may prescribe forms which shall be used in connection therewith.

None of the functions, powers or duties enumerated in Sections 14, 18, and 31 and paragraphs (a) and (j) of Section 20 of this Act shall be exercised by the Department except upon the action and report in writing of the Board.

SECTION 10. There shall be in the Department a Commissioner of Real Estate appointed by the Director who shall hold a currently valid broker's license, which shall be placed on inactive status during such appointment. The Commissioner shall report to the Director and shall have the following duties:

(1) Act as Chairperson of the Board, ex-officio, without vote;

(2) Be the direct liaison between the Department, the profession and real estate organizations and associations;

(3) Prepare and circulate to licensees such educational and informational material as the Department deems necessary for guidance or assistance to licensees;

(4) Cause to be investigated actions of any person, firm or corporation and such of the records thereof as are connected with the transfer, sale, rental or lease of real property;

(5) Appoint any necessary committees to assist in the performance of the Department's functions and duties under this Act; and

(6) Subject to the administrative approval of the Director, supervise the real estate unit of the Department.

In designating the Commissioner of Real Estate, the Director shall give due consideration to recommendations by members and organizations of the profession.

SECTION 11. Every person who desires to obtain a license shall make application to the Department in writing upon blanks prepared and furnished by the Department. Each application shall contain evidence that the applicant is at least 21 years of age, evidence of the honesty, truthfulness and integrity of the applicant, evidence that the applicant has successfully completed a 4 year course of study in a high school or secondary school approved by the Illinois State Board of Education or an equivalent course of study as determined by an examination conducted by the Illinois State Board of Education and shall be verified under oath by the applicant.

When an applicant has had his license revoked on prior occasion or when an applicant is found to have committed any of the practices enumerated in Section 18 hereof during the term of his prior licensure or when an applicant has been convicted of forgery, embezzlement, obtaining money under false pretenses, larceny, extortion, conspiracy to defraud, or any other similar offense or offenses, or has been convicted of a felony involving moral turpitude in any court of competent jurisdiction in this or any other state, district or territory of the United States, or of a foreign country, the Board may consider such prior revocation, conduct or conviction the Board shall take into account the nature of the offense, any aggravating or extenuating circumstances, the time elapsed since such revocation, conduct or conviction, the rehabilitation or restitution performed by the applicant and such other factors as the Board deems relevant. The Board may in its discretion deny a license to any person who has engaged in a licensed real estate activity without a license. When an applicant has made a false statement of material fact on his application, such false statement may in itself be sufficient grounds to revoke or refuse to issue a license.

All applicants for a broker's license, except applicants who have been admitted to practice law by the Supreme Court of Illinois, shall have first served actively for one year of the last 3 prior years as a salesperson and give satisfactory evidence of having completed at least 90 classroom hours in real estate courses approved by the Board or in lieu thereof a correspondence course approved by the Board or show evidence of receiving a baccalaureate degree including at least minor courses involving real estate or related material from a college or university approved by the Board, and all such applicants shall satisfactorily pass a written examination as provided for in this Act.

All applicants for a salesperson's license, except applicants who have been admitted to practice law by the Supreme Court of Illinois, shall show evidence satisfactory to the Board that they have completed at least 30 hours of instruction in real estate courses approved by the Board or in lieu thereof a correspondence course approved by the Board, and satisfactorily pass a written examination as provided for in this Act. The minimum age of 21 years may be waived to any person seeking a license as a real estate salesperson who has attained the age of 18 and can provide evidence of the successful completion of at least 2 years past secondary school study, with major emphasis on real estate courses, in a school approved by the Department.

SECTION 12. (a) Every person who makes application for an original license as a broker or salesperson shall personally take a written examination authorized by the Department, and answer such questions as may be required by the Department to determine the trustworthiness of the applicant, and the applicant's competency to transact the business of broker or salesperson, as the case may be, in such a manner as to safeguard the interests of the public. In determining such competency, the Department shall require proof that the applicant has a good understanding and the knowledge to conduct real estate brokerage and of the provisions of this Act. The examination shall be prepared by the Board or by an independent testing service designated by the Board subject to the approval of the tests by the Board. The Board or its designated independent testing service shall conduct such examinations at such times and places as the Board shall approve. In addi-

154 ILLINOIS SUPPLEMENT for Modern Real Estate Practice

tion, every person who desires to take such written examination, shall make application to do so to the Department or to the designated independent testing service in writing upon the forms approved by the Department. An applicant shall be eligible to take such examination only after fulfilling the following requirements:

(1) successfully completing the education requirements, and

(2) attaining the minimum age specified in this Act.

Each applicant shall be required to establish compliance with such eligibility requirements in the manner provided by the rules and regulations promulgated for the administration of this Act.

(b) If a person who has successfully completed the written examination hereinbefore described fails to file an application for a license under this Act within one year after successfully completing such examination, credit for successful completion of such examination shall be denied. Such person thereafter may make a new application for examination.

(c) No successful applicant shall engage in any of the activities covered by this Act until a license has been issued to such applicant or the applicant has received a letter from the Department authorizing such activities pending receipt of a license.

(d) No licensee shall accept a commission or valuable consideration for the performance of any of the activities herein specified from any person, except the licensee's employer, a broker licensed under this Act.

(e) The Department shall issue to each applicant entitled thereto, a license in such form and size as shall be prescribed by the Department. The person to whom such a license is issued is hereafter designated a "licensee". Each license shall bear the name of the licensee as the person so qualified, shall specify whether such person is qualified to act in a broker, associate broker or salesperson capacity, and shall contain

such other matter as shall be recommended by the Board and approved by the Department. Each person licensed under this Act shall display his own license conspicuously in his place of business.

SECTION 13. The expiration date and renewal period for each license issued under this Act shall be set by rule. The holder of a license may renew such license during the month preceding the expiration date thereof by paying the required fee. However, any licensee whose license has expired while engaged in (1) federal service on active duty with the Army of the United States, the United States Navy, the Marine Corps, the United States Air Force, the Coast Guard, or the State Militia called into the service or training of the United States of America, or (2) training or education under the supervision of the United States preliminary to induction into the military service, or (3) serving as Commissioner of Real Estate, may have his license renewed without paying any lapsed renewal fee or reinstatement fee if, within 2 years after termination of such service, training or education other than by dishonorable discharge, the licensee furnishes the Department with an affidavit to the effect that the licensee has been so engaged and that such service, training or education has been so terminated.

The revocation, suspension, termination or expiration of a broker's license shall automatically suspend every salesperson's and associate broker's sponsor card granted to any person by virtue of their employment by or association with such broker and such suspension shall continue until the broker's license shall have been reinstated or renewed. A salesperson or associate broker changing employment or association to another broker shall be authorized to continue to practice upon the issuance of a new sponsor card by the new broker.

The Department shall establish and maintain a register of all licensees currently licensed by the State and shall issue and prescribe a form of pocket card. Upon payment by a licensee of an appropriate fee as prescribed in Section 15 of this Act for active engagement in the activity for which the licensee is qualified and who holds a license for the current period, the Department shall issue a pocket card to such licensee. The pocket card shall verify that the required fee for the current period has been paid and shall indicate that the person named thereon is licensed for the current year as a broker, associate broker or salesperson, as the case may be. The pocket card shall further indicate that the licensee named thereon is authorized by the Department to engage in the licensed activity appropriate for his status (broker, associate broker or salesperson) only when such pocket card is accompanied by the required sponsor card. Each licensee shall carry on his person his pocket card accompanied by the required sponsor card when engaging in any licensed activity and shall display the same on demand.

The broker shall prepare upon forms provided by the Department and deliver to each salesperson or associate broker employed by or associated with the broker a sponsor card certifying that the person whose name appears thereon is in fact employed by or associated with said broker. The broker shall send a duplicate of each such sponsor card to the Department within 24 hours of issuance. It is a violation of this Act for any broker to issue a sponsor card to any salesperson or associate broker unless such salesperson or associate broker presents in hand an active license as provided for herein. The sponsor card shall remain at all times the property of the broker. Each salesperson and associate broker shall carry on their person their sponsor card accompanied by the required pocket card when engaging in any licensed activity and shall display the same on demand.

Upon changing place of business, the broker shall immediately notify the Department in writing of such change. The broker shall immediately after a change in place of business prepare and deliver new sponsor cards to all associate brokers and salespersons employed by or associated with such broker. The broker shall send a duplicate of each such sponsor card to the Department within 24 hours of issuance.

When a salesperson or associate broker terminates his employment or association with a broker, or is terminated by such broker, such salesperson or associate broker shall return to that broker the sponsor card issued by that broker by hand delivery or by registered or certified mail, return receipt requested, all within 24 hours from the time of such termination. It is a violation of this Act for any salesperson or associate broker to accept employment or association with another broker unless having first complied with the termination provisions of this Section. That broker shall surrender to the Department the sponsor card returned by such salesperson or associate broker within 2 days of its return or shall notify the Department in writing of such termination and explain why such card is not surrendered.

To change status from an associate broker to broker, the associate broker shall make application to the Department and pay the required fee. Upon compliance with all of the provisions of this Section the Department shall issue the associate broker a broker's license and upon receipt thereof the associate broker shall terminate his relationship with the sponsoring broker in accordance with this Section.

When a broker is required under this Act to send to the Department a duplicate sponsor card, such broker shall send the duplicate sponsor card by registered or certified mail, return receipt requested, and shall pay the fee prescribed in Section 15 of this Act to the Department to cover administrative expenses attendant to the changes in the register of the licensee.

If a broker maintains more than one place of business within the State, a branch office license shall be issued to such broker for each branch office so maintained, and the branch office license shall be displayed conspicuously in each branch office. The manager of a branch office shall be a broker or associate broker and must be closely supervised by the employing broker. However, no broker or associate broker shall be permitted to be in direct operational control of more than one office or branch office.

Any licensee who is a resident of Illinois and who desires to become inactive, may apply for and receive a license as an inactive broker, inactive associate broker or inactive salesperson if the licensee continues to reside in the State of Illinois.

No licensee shall engage in, carry on, or advertise as being actively engaged in the real estate business so long as the licensee occupies the status of a licensed inactive broker, inactive associate broker or inactive salesperson. If any licensee continues his inactive status or allows his license to lapse for a period of more than 5 but less than 7 years, the licensee shall not be entitled to re-register as an active broker, associate broker or salesperson until first providing evidence of satisfactory completion of at least 15 hours of refresher courses in real estate subjects at a school approved by the Department. Any license which has lapsed for 7 consecutive years from the last expiration date of such license cannot be renewed or reinstated after the completion of that 7 year period.

SECTION 14. A nonresident of this State, who is actively engaged in the real estate business as a broker and who maintains a place of business in his resident state which borders this State, and who has been duly licensed in such bordering state to conduct such business in that state, such state having entered into a reciprocal agreement with the Department in regard to the issuance of reciprocal licenses, and who meets all the other requirements of this Act, may be issued a nonresident broker's license.

Such nonresident broker's license may be issued by the Department without examination to a broker licensed under the laws of another state of the United States which borders this State under the following conditions: (1) the broker holds a broker's license in his home state; (2) the standards for that state for registration as a broker are substantially equivalent to the minimum standards in the State of Illinois; (3) has been actively practicing as a broker in the resident state for a period of not less than 2 years, immediately prior to the date of application; (4) the broker furnishes the Department with a statement under seal of the proper authority in real estate licensure of the state in which the broker is licensed showing that said broker has an active broker's license, is in good standing and no complaints are pending against the broker, in that state.

Illinois Real Estate License Act of 1983 • Page 15

A nonresident salesperson employed by or associated with a broker holding a nonresident broker's license may in the discretion of the Department be issued, without examination, a nonresident salesperson's license under such nonresident broker. The nonresident broker shall comply with the provisions of this Act and issue said salesperson a sponsor card upon the form provided by the Department.

Prior to the issuance of a license to a nonresident broker or salesperson, such broker or salesperson shall file with the Department a designation in writing that appoints the Director to act as his agent upon whom all judicial and other process or legal notices directed to such licensee may be served. Service upon the agent so designated shall be equivalent to personal service upon the licensee. Copies of such appointment, certified by the Director, shall be deemed sufficient evidence thereof and shall be admitted in evidence with the same force and effect as the original thereof might be admitted. In such written designation, the licensee shall agree that any lawful process against the licensee which is served upon such agent shall be of the same legal force and validity as if served upon the licensee, and that the authority shall continue in force so long as any liability remains outstanding in this State. Upon the receipt of any such process or notice, the Director shall forthwith mail a copy of the same by certified mail to the last known business address of the licensee.

As a condition precedent to the issuance of a license to a nonresident broker or salesperson, such broker or salesperson shall agree in writing to abide by all the provisions of this Act with respect to his real estate activities within the State of Illinois and submit to the jurisdiction of the Department as provided in this Act. Such agreement shall be filed with the Department and shall remain in force for so long as the nonresident broker or salesperson is licensed by this State and thereafter with respect to acts or omissions committed while licensed as a nonresident broker or salesperson.

Prior to the issuance of any license to any nonresident, a duly certified copy of the license issued for the conducting of such

Page 16 • *Illinois Real Estate License Act of 1983*

business in any other state must be filed with the Department by such nonresident, and the same fees must be paid as provided in this Act for the obtaining of a broker's or salesperson's license in this State.

Nonresident licenses granted under reciprocal agreements as provided in this Section shall remain in force, unless suspended or revoked or terminated by the Department for just cause or for failure to pay the required renewal fee, only as long as the reciprocal agreement is in effect between this State and the resident state of the licensee.

SECTION 15. The following fees, which are not refundable except as provided in this Section, shall be paid to the Department for the functions performed by the Department under this Act:

(A) License of real estate salesperson.

(1) The fee for a license as a salesperson is $39, of which $25 is a processing fee, $10 is a fee for the Real Estate Recovery Fund as provided by Section 23, and $4 is a fee for deposit in the Real Estate Research and Education Fund for use as provided in Section 16. The processing fee, the Recovery Fund fee and the Real Estate Research and Education Fund fee must accompany the application to determine the applicant's fitness to receive a license. In the event the applicant is ineligible for a license, the Recovery Fund fee and the Real Estate Research and Education Fund fee will be returned to the applicant, and the processing fee shall be forfeited to the Department.

(2) The fee for renewal of a license as a salesperson shall be calculated at the rate of $5 per year.

(3) The fee for the reinstatement of a license as a salesperson which has expired for not more than 7 years is $29, plus all lapsed renewal fees, of which $4 is a fee for deposit in the Real Estate Research and Education Fund for use as provided in Section 16, and $10 is a fee for deposit in the Real Estate Recovery Fund for use as provided in Section 23.

(4) The fee for a license as an inactive salesperson is $10.

(5) The fee for a license as a salesperson following a period of registration as an inactive salesperson is $34, of which $20 is a processing fee, $4 is a fee for deposit in the Real Estate Research and Education Fund for use as provided in Section 16, and $10 is a fee for deposit in the Real Estate Recovery Fund for use as provided in Section 22.

(B) License of Broker or Associate Broker.

(1) The fee for a license as a broker or associate broker is $64, of which $50 is a processing fee, $10 is a fee for the Real Estate Recovery Fund, as provided by Section 23 and $4 is a fee for deposit in the Real Estate Research and Education Fund for use as provided in Section 16. The processing fee, the Recovery Fund fee and the Real Estate Research and Education Fund fee must accompany the application to determine an applicant's fitness to receive a license. In the event the applicant is ineligible for a license the Recovery Fund fee and the Real Estate Research and Education Fund fee shall be returned to the applicant, and the processing fee shall be forfeited to the Department.

(2) The fee for the renewal of a license as a broker or associate broker shall be calculated at the rate of $10 per year.

(3) The fee for the reinstatement of a license as a broker or associate broker which has expired for not more than 7 years is $39, plus all lapsed renewal fees, of which $4 is a fee for deposit in the Real Estate Research and Education Fund for use as provided in Section 16, and $10 is a fee for deposit in the Real Estate Recovery Fund for use as provided in Section 23.

(4) The fee for a license as an inactive broker or inactive associate broker is $15.

(5) The fee for a license as a broker or associate broker following a period of registration in inactive status is $44, of which $30 is a processing fee, $4 is a fee for deposit in the Real Estate Research and Education Fund for use as provided in Section 16, and $10 is a fee for deposit in the Real Estate Recovery Fund for use as provided in Section 23.

(C) License of partnership or corporation.

(1) The fee for a license for a partnership or corporation is $54, of which $40 is a processing fee, $4 is a fee for deposit in the Real Estate Research and Education Fund for use as provided in Section 16, and $10 is a fee for deposit in the Real Estate Recovery Fund for use as provided in Section 23.

(2) The fee for the renewal of a license for a partnership or corporation shall be calculated at the rate of $20 per year.

(D) Real Estate School and Instructor Fees.

(1) The fee for an application for initial approval of a private, business or vocational real estate school is $600.

(2) The fee for renewal of such approval shall be calculated at the rate of $300 per year.

(3) The fee for an application for initial approval of a branch for a private, business or vocational real estate school is $100 per branch.

(4) The fee for renewal of such approval shall be calculated at the rate of $50 per branch.

(5) The fee for transferring a branch location shall be $10 per transfer.

(6) The fee for application for initial approval of a private, business or vocational real estate school instructor is $15.

(7) The fee for renewal of such approval for that instructor shall be calculated at the rate of $10 per year.

(E) General Fees.

(1) The fee for the issuance of a duplicate license or pocket card, for the issuance of a replacement license or pocket card which has been lost or destroyed, for the issuance of a license with a change of name or address other than during the renewal period, or for the issuance of a license with a change of location of business is $10. No fee is required for name and address changes on Department records when no duplicate license is issued.

(2) The fee for a certification of a licensee's record for any purpose is $10.

(3) The fee for a wall license showing registration shall be the cost of producing such license. Such fees shall be deposited by the Department into the Department of Central Management Services Printing Revolving Fund.

(4) The fee for a roster of persons licensed as brokers, associate brokers or salespersons in this State shall be the cost of producing such a roster.

(5) The fee for a license for a branch office is $10.

(6) The fee for the renewal of a branch office license shall be calculated at the rate of $10 per year.

(7) Applicants for an examination as a broker or salesperson shall be required to pay, either to the Department or to the designated testing service, a fee covering the cost of providing the examination. Failure to appear for the examination on the scheduled date, at the time

and place specified, after the applicant's application for examination has been received and acknowledged by the Department or the designated testing service, shall result in the forfeiture of the examination fee.

(8) The fee for recording a duplicate sponsor card is $10.

(9) The fee for furnishing a record of proceedings provided for in subsection (h) of Section 20 of this Act or for certifying the record referred to in Section 21 of this Act is $1 per page of the transcript.

SECTION 16. A special fund to be known as the Real Estate Research and Education Fund is created in the State Treasury. All money deposited in such special fund shall be used only for the ordinary and contingent expenses of operation of the Office of Real Estate Research or its successor, by whatever name designated, at the University of Illinois.

Moneys in the Real Estate Research and Education Fund may be invested and reinvested in the same manner as funds in the Real Estate Recovery Fund. All earnings received from such investment shall be deposited in the Real Estate Research and Education Fund and may be used for the same purposes as fees deposited in such fund.

SECTION 17. All fees received by the Department under this Act, other than fees which this Act directs to be deposited in the Real Estate Recovery Fund, in the Real Estate Research and Education Fund or in the Department of Central Management Services Printing Revolving Fund, shall be deposited in a special fund in the State Treasury to be known as the Real Estate License Administration Fund. The moneys deposited in the Real Estate License Administration Fund shall be appropriated to the Department for expenses of the Department and the Board in the administration of this Act and for the administration of any Act administered by the Department providing revenue to this Fund.

The Director shall employ, in conformity with the Personnel Code, one full time Chief of Real Estate Investigations; and the Director shall also employ, in conformity with the Personnel Code, not less than one full time investigator and one full time auditor for every 15,000 licensees registered under this Act.

The Chief of Real Estate Investigations shall be a college graduate from an accredited 4 year college or university with 3 years' responsible administrative experience and a minimum of 3 years' responsible investigatory experience in law enforcement or a related field.

Moneys in the Real Estate License Administration Fund may be invested and reinvested in the same manner as funds in the Real Estate Recovery Fund. All earnings received from such investment shall be deposited in the Real Estate License Administration Fund and may be used for the same purposes as fees deposited in such fund.

Upon the completion of any audit of the Department, as prescribed by the Illinois State Auditing Act, which includes an audit of the Real Estate License Administration Fund, the Department shall make the audit open to inspection by any interested person.

SECTION 18. The Department may refuse to issue or renew, may suspend or may revoke any license, or may censure, reprimand or impose a civil penalty not to exceed $10,000 upon any licensee hereunder for any one or any combination of the following causes:

(a) Where the applicant or licensee has, by false or fraudulent representation, obtained or sought to obtain a license.

(b) Where the licensee has been convicted of any crime, an essential element of which is dishonesty or fraud or larceny, embezzlement, obtaining money, property or credit by false pretenses or by means of a confidence game, has been convicted in this or another state of a crime which is a felony under the laws of this State or has been convicted of a felony in a federal court.

(c) Where the licensee has been adjudged to be subject to involuntary admission or to meet the standard for judicial admission as provided in the Mental Health and Developmental Disabilities Code, as now or hereafter amended.

(d) Where the applicant or licensee performs or attempts to perform any act as a broker or salesperson in a retail sales establishment, from an office, desk or space that is not separated from the main retail business by a separate and distinct area within such establishment.

(e) Where the licensee in performing or attempting to perform or pretending to perform any act as a broker or salesperson, or where such licensee, in handling his own property, whether held by deed, option, or otherwise, is found guilty of:

1. Making any substantial misrepresentation, or untruthful advertising;

2. Making any false promises of a character likely to influence, persuade, or induce;

3. Pursuing a continued and flagrant course of misrepresentation or the making of false promises through agents, salespersons or advertising or otherwise;

4. Any misleading or untruthful advertising, or using any trade name or insignia of membership in any real estate organization of which the licensee is not a member;

5. Acting for more than one party in a transaction without the written acknowledgement of all parties for whom the licensee acts;

6. Representing or attempting to represent a broker other than the employer;

7. Failure to account for or to remit for any moneys or documents coming into their possession which belong to others;

8. Failure to maintain and deposit in a special account, separate and apart from a personal or other business account, all moneys belonging to others entrusted to the licensee while acting as a broker, or as escrow agent, or as the temporary custodian of the funds of others until the transaction involved is consummated or terminated; such account shall be noninterest bearing unless the character of the deposit is such that interest thereon is otherwise required by law, or unless written agreement of the principals to the transaction requires that the deposit be placed in an interest bearing account;

9. Failing to furnish copies upon request of all documents relating to a real estate transaction to all parties executing them;

10. Paying a commission or valuable consideration to any person for acts or services performed in violation of this Act;

11. Having demonstrated unworthiness or incompetency to act as a broker, associate broker or salesperson in such manner as to endanger the interest of the public;

12. Commingling the money or property of others with his own;

13. Employing any person as a salesperson or associate broker on a purely temporary or single deal basis as a means of evading the law regarding payment of commission to nonlicensees on some contemplated transactions;

14. Permitting the use of his license as a broker to enable a salesperson to operate a real estate business without actual participation therein and control thereof by the broker;

15. Any other conduct, whether of the same or a different character from that specified in this Section which constitutes dishonest dealing;

chase or sales plan whereby a broker enters into a conditional or unconditional written contract with a seller by the terms of which a broker agrees to purchase a property of the seller within a specified period of time at a specific price in the event the property is not sold in accordance with the terms of a listing contract between the broker and the seller or on other terms acceptable to the seller;

(B) A broker offering a "guaranteed sales plan" shall provide the details and conditions of such plan in writing to the party to whom the plan is offered;

(C) A broker offering a "guaranteed sales plan" shall provide to the party to whom the plan is offered, evidence of sufficient financial resources to satisfy the commitment to purchase undertaken by the broker in the plan;

(D) Any broker offering a "guaranteed sales plan" shall undertake to market the property of the seller subject to the plan in the same manner in which the broker would market any other property, unless such agreement with the seller provides otherwise;

(E) Any broker who fails to perform on a "guaranteed sales plan" in strict accordance with its terms shall be subject to all the penalties provided in this Act for violations thereof, and, in addition, shall be subject to a civil penalty payable to the party injured by the default in an amount of up to $10,000;

21. Influencing or attempting to influence by any words or acts a prospective seller, purchaser, occupant, landlord or tenant of real estate, in connection with viewing, buying or leasing of real estate, so as to promote, or tend to promote, the continuance or maintenance of racially and religiously segregated housing, or so as to retard, obstruct or discourage racially integrated housing on or in any street, block, neighborhood or community;

16. Displaying a "for rent" or "for sale" sign on any property without the written consent of an owner or his duly authorized agent, or advertising that any property is for sale or for rent in a newspaper or other publication without the consent of the owner or his authorized agent;

17. Failing to provide information requested by the Department, within 30 days of the request, either as the result of a formal or informal complaint to the Department or as a result of a random audit conducted by the Department, which would indicate a violation of this Act;

18. Disregarding or violating any provision of this Act, or the published rules or regulations promulgated by the Department to enforce this Act;

19. Advertising any property for sale or advertising any transaction of any kind or character relating to the sale of property by whatsoever means, without clearly disclosing in such advertising one of the following: the name of the firm with which the licensee is associated, if a sole broker evidence of the broker's occupation, or a name with respect to which the broker has complied with the requirements of "An Act in relation to the use of an assumed name in the conduct or transaction of business in this State", approved July 17, 1941, as amended, whether such advertising is done by the broker or by any salesperson or associate broker employed by the broker;

20. Using prizes, money, free gifts or other valuable consideration as inducements to (1) secure customers to purchase, rent or lease property when the awarding of such prizes, money, free gifts or other valuable consideration is conditioned upon such purchase, rental or lease, or (2) secure clients to list properties with licensee; this paragraph 20 shall not be construed to apply to "guaranteed sales plans", as defined in subparagraph (A) except to the extent hereinafter set forth:

(A) A "guaranteed sales plan" is any real estate pur-

22. Engaging in any act which constitutes a violation of Section 3-102, 3-103, 3-104, or 3-105 of the Illinois Human Rights Act, whether or not a complaint has been filed with or adjudicated by the Human Rights Commission;

23. Inducing any party to a contract of sale to break such a contract for the purpose of substituting, in lieu thereof, a new contract with a third party.

24. Negotiating a sale, exchange or lease of real property directly with an owner or lessor without authority from the listing broker if the licensee knows that the owner or lessor has a written exclusive listing agreement covering the property with another broker.

25. Where a licensee, who is also a lawyer, acts as the lawyer for either the buyer or the seller in the same transaction in which such licensee is acting or has acted as a broker or salesperson.

SECTION 19. No licensee shall obtain any written listing contract which does not provide for automatic expiration within a definite period of time. No notice of termination at the final expiration thereof shall be required. Any listing contract not containing a provision for automatic expiration shall be void.

SECTION 20.
(a) The Department may conduct hearings on proceedings to suspend, revoke or to refuse to issue or renew licenses of persons applying for licensure or licensed under this Act, or to censure, reprimand or impose a civil penalty not to exceed $10,000 upon any licensee hereunder and may revoke, suspend or refuse to issue or renew such licenses or censure, reprimand or impose a civil penalty not to exceed $10,000 upon any licensee hereunder.

(b) Upon the motion of either the Department or the Board or upon the verified complaint in writing of any persons setting forth facts which if proven would constitute grounds for suspension or revocation under Section 18 of this Act, the Board shall investigate the actions of any person so accused who holds or represents to hold a license. Such person is hereinafter called the accused.

(c) The Department shall, before suspending, revoking, placing on probationary status, or taking any other disciplinary action as the Department may deem proper with regard to any license: (1) notify the accused in writing at least 30 days prior to the date set for the hearing of any charges made and the time and place for a hearing of the charges to be heard before the Board under oath; and (2) inform the accused that upon failure to file an answer and request a hearing before the date originally set for such hearing, default will be taken against the accused and his license may be suspended, revoked, placed on probationary status, or other disciplinary action, including limiting the scope, nature or extent of the accused's practice, as the Department may deem proper, may be taken with regard thereto.

(d) At the time and place fixed in the notice, the Board shall proceed to hearing of the charges and both the accused person and the complainant shall be accorded ample opportunity to present in person or by counsel such statements, testimony, evidence and argument as may be pertinent to the charges or to any defense thereto. The Board may continue such hearing from time to time. If the Board shall not be sitting at the time and place fixed in the notice or at the time and place to which the hearing shall have been continued, the Department shall continue such hearing for a period not to exceed 30 days.

(e) Any unlawful act or violation of any of the provisions of this Act upon the part of any salesperson, associate broker or unlicensed employee of a licensed broker, shall not be cause for the revocation of the license of any such broker, partial or otherwise, unless it appears to the satisfaction of the Department that the broker had knowledge thereof.

(f) The Department or Board has power to subpoena and bring before it any person in this State and to take testimony either orally or by deposition, or both, with the same fees and mileage and in the same manner as prescribed by law in judicial procedure in civil cases in courts of this State.

The Director, Commissioner of Real Estate and any member of the Board shall each have power to administer oaths to witnesses at any hearing which the Department is authorized by law to conduct, and any other oaths required or authorized in any Act administered by the Department.

(g) Any circuit court or any judge thereof, upon the application of the accused person or complainant or the Department or Board, may, by order entered, require the attendance of witnesses and the production of relevant books and papers before the Board in any hearing relative to the application for or refusal, recall, suspension or revocation of a license, and the court or judge may compel obedience to the court's and the judge's order by proceedings for contempt.

(h) The Department, at its expense, shall preserve a record of all proceedings at the formal hearing of any case involving the refusal to issue or the revocation, suspension or other discipline of a licensee. The notice of hearing, complaint and all other documents in the nature of pleadings and written motions filed in the proceedings, the transcript of testimony, the report of the Board and the orders of the Department shall be the record of such proceeding.

(i) The Board shall present to the Director its written report of its findings and recommendations. A copy of such report shall be served upon the accused person, either personally or by registered mail as provided in this Act for the service of the citation. Within 20 days after such service, the accused person may present to the Director a motion in writing for a rehearing which shall specify the particular grounds therefor. If the accused person shall order and pay for a transcript of the record as provided in this Act, the time elapsing thereafter and before such transcript is ready for delivery to the accused shall not be counted as part of such 20 days.

Whenever the Director is satisfied that substantial justice has not been done, the Director may order a rehearing by the Board or other special committee appointed by the Director. In all instances, under this Act, in which the Board has rendered a recommendation to the Director with respect to a particular registrant, the Director shall, in the event that he disagrees with or takes action contrary to the recommendation of the Board, file with the Board and the Secretary of State his specific written reasons of disagreement with the Board. Such reasons shall be filed within 30 days of the Board's recommendation to the Director and prior to any contrary action. At the expiration of the time specified for filing a motion for a rehearing the Director shall have the right to take the action recommended by the Board. Upon the suspension or revocation of a license, the licensee shall be required to surrender their license to the Department, and upon failure or refusal so to do, the Department shall have the right to seize such license.

(j) At any time after the suspension or revocation of any license, the Department may restore it to the accused person without examination, upon the written recommendation of the Board.

(k) An order or revocation or suspension or a certified copy thereof, over the seal of the Department and purporting to be signed by the Director, shall be prima facie proof that:

1. Such signature is the genuine signature of the Director;

2. Such Director is duly appointed and qualified;

3. The Board and the members thereof are qualified.

Such proof may be rebutted.

SECTION 21. All final administrative decisions of the Department shall be subject to judicial review pursuant to the provisions of the Administrative Review Law, and all amendments and modifications thereof, and the rules adopted pursuant thereto. The term "administrative decision" is defined in Section 3-101 of the Administrative Review Law.

The Department shall not be required to certify any record or file any answer or otherwise appear unless the party filing the complaint pays to the Department the certification fee provided for in Section 15 representing costs of such certification. Failure on the part of the plaintiff to make such a deposit shall be grounds for dismissal of the action.

SECTION 22. Any person or corporation violating any provision of this Act other than Section 18, subsection (e), paragraph 4, and other than Section 3, or any person or corporation failing to account for or to remit for any moneys commingling the money or other property of his or its principal with his or its own, upon conviction for the first offense, is guilty of a Class C misdemeanor, and if a corporation, is guilty of a business offense and shall be fined not to exceed $2000.

Upon conviction of a second or subsequent offense the violator, if a person, is guilty of a Class A misdemeanor; and if a corporation, is guilty of a business offense and shall be fined not less than $2000 nor more than $5000.

Any person or corporation violating any provision of Section 3 of this Act, upon conviction for the first offense, is guilty of a Class A misdemeanor, and if a corporation, is guilty of a business offense and shall be fined not to exceed $10,000.

Upon conviction of a second or subsequent offense the violator, if a person, is guilty of a Class 4 felony; and if a corporation, is guilty of a business offense and shall be fined not less than $10,000 nor more than $25,000.

Any officer or agent of a corporation, or member or agent of a partnership who shall personally participate in or be accessory to any violation of this Act by such corporation or partnership shall be subject to the penalties herein prescribed for individuals; and the State's Attorney of the county where such offense is committed shall prosecute all persons violating the provisions of this Act upon proper complaint being made.

All fines and penalties shall be deposited in the Real Estate Recovery Fund in the State Treasury.

The Department shall have the duty and the right on behalf of the People of the State of Illinois to originate injunction proceedings against any person acting or purporting to act as a broker, associate broker, or salesperson without a license issued under the provisions of this Act. The Department shall also have the duty and the right on behalf of the People of the State of Illinois to originate injunction proceedings against any licensee to enjoin acts by the licensee which constitute violations of this Act.

SECTION 23. The Department shall establish and maintain a Real Estate Recovery Fund from which any person aggrieved by an act, representation, transaction, or conduct of a duly licensed broker, associate broker, salesperson, or unlicensed employee, which is in violation of this Act or the regulations promulgated pursuant thereto, or which constitutes embezzlement of money or property, or money or property unlawfully obtained from any person by false pretenses, artifice, trickery or forgery or by reason of any fraud, misrepresentation, discrimination or deceit by or on the part of any such licensee or the unlicensed employee of any such broker, and which results in a loss of actual cash money as opposed to losses in market value, may recover. Such aggrieved person may recover by order of the circuit court of the county where the violation occurred, an amount of not more than $10,000 from such fund for damages sustained by the act, representation, transaction, or conduct, together with costs of suit and attorneys' fees incurred in connection therewith of not to exceed 15% of the amount of the recovery ordered paid from such Fund. However, no licensed broker, associate broker or salesperson may recover from the fund unless the court finds that the person suffered a loss resulting from intentional misconduct. Such court order shall not include interest on the judgment.

The maximum liability against such Fund arising out of any one act shall be as provided in this Section and the judgment order shall spread the award equitably among all co-owners or otherwise aggrieved persons, if any. The maximum liability against such Fund arising out of the activities of any single broker, any single associate broker, any single salesperson, or any single unlicensed employee, since January 1, 1974, shall be the sum of $50,000.

Nothing in this Section shall be construed to authorize recovery from the Real Estate Recovery Fund unless the loss of the aggrieved person results from an act or omission of a duly licensed broker, associate broker, salesperson or unlicensed employee who was at the time of the act or omission acting in such capacity or was apparently acting in such capacity, and unless the aggrieved person has obtained a valid judgment as provided in Section 25.

Any person who makes application for an original license to practice as a broker, associate broker, or salesperson shall pay, in addition to the original fee, a fee prescribed in Section 15 of this Act for deposit in the Real Estate Recovery Fund. If the Department does not issue the license, this fee shall be returned to the applicant.

SECTION 24. If, on December 31 of any year, the balance remaining in the Real Estate Recovery Fund is less than $1,250,000, every broker and associate broker, when renewing his license, at the next regular renewal time, shall pay, in addition to his renewal fee, a fee of $10 for deposit in the Real Estate Recovery Fund, and every salesperson, when renewing his license, at the next regular renewal time, shall pay, in addition to their renewal fee, a fee of $10 for deposit in the Real Estate Recovery Fund.

SECTION 25.
(a) No action for a judgment which subsequently results in an order for collection from the Real Estate Recovery Fund shall be started later than 2 years from the accrual of the cause of action thereon. When any aggrieved person commences action for a judgment which may result in collection from the Real Estate Recovery Fund, the aggrieved person shall notify the Department in writing to this effect at the time of the commencement of such action. When any aggrieved person commences action for a judgment which may result in collection from the Real Estate Recovery Fund, and the aggrieved person is unable to obtain legal and proper service upon the defendant under the provisions of Illinois law concerning service of process in civil actions, the aggrieved person may petition the Court where the action to obtain judgment was begun for an order to allow service of legal process on the Director. Service of process on the Director shall be taken and held in that court to be as valid and binding as if due service had been made upon the defendant. In case any process mentioned in this Section is served upon the Director, the Director shall forward a copy of the process by registered mail to the licensee's last address on record with the Department. Any judgment obtained after service of process on the Director under this Act shall apply to and be enforceable against the Real Estate Recovery Fund only. The Department may intervene in and defend any such action.

(b) The aggrieved person shall give written notice to the Department within 30 days of the entry of any judgment which may result in collection from the Real Estate Recovery Fund. Such aggrieved person shall provide the Department within 20 days prior written notice of all supplementary proceedings so as to allow the Department to participate in all efforts to collect on the judgment.

(c) When any aggrieved person recovers a valid judgment in any court of competent jurisdiction against any licensee, or an unlicensed employee of any broker, upon the grounds of fraud, misrepresentation, discrimination or deceit, the aggrieved person may, upon the termination of all proceedings, including review and appeals in connection with the judgment, file a verified claim in the court in which the judgment was entered and, upon 30 days' written notice to the Department, and to the person against whom the judgment was obtained, may apply to the court for an order directing payment out of the Real Estate Recovery Fund, of the amount unpaid upon the judgment, not including interest on such judgment, and subject to the limitations stated in Section 23 of this Act. The court shall proceed to an evidentiary hearing on the application, and upon the hearing thereof, the aggrieved person shall be required to show that such aggrieved person:

1) is not a spouse of debtor, or the personal representative of such spouse.

2) has complied with all the requirements of this Section.

3) has obtained a judgment stating the amount thereof and the amount owing thereon, not including interest thereon, at the date of the application.

4) has made all reasonable searches and inquiries to ascertain whether the judgment debtor is possessed of real or personal property or other assets, liable to be sold or applied in satisfaction of the judgment.

5) by such search has discovered no personal or real property or other assets liable to be sold or applied, or has discovered certain of them, describing them owned by the judgment debtor and liable to be so applied, and has taken all necessary action and proceedings for the realization thereof, and the amount thereby realized was insufficient to satisfy the judgment, stating the amount so realized and the balance remaining due on the judgment after application of the amount realized.

6) has diligently pursued all remedies against all the judgment debtors and all other persons liable to the aggrieved person in the transaction for which recovery is sought from the Real Estate Recovery Fund.

The aggrieved person shall also be required to prove the amount of attorney's fees sought to be recovered and the reasonableness of those fees up to the maximum allowed pursuant to Section 23 of this Act.

(d) The court shall make an order directed to the Department requiring payment from the Real Estate Recovery Fund of whatever sum it finds to be payable upon the claim, pursuant to and in accordance with the limitations contained in Section 23, if the court is satisfied, upon the hearing, of the truth of all matters required to be shown by the aggrieved person by subsection (b) of this Section and that the aggrieved person has fully pursued and exhausted all remedies available for recovering the amount awarded by the judgment of the court.

(e) Should the Department pay from the Real Estate Recovery Fund any amount in settlement of a claim or toward satisfaction of a judgment against a licensed broker, associate broker or salesperson, or an unlicensed employee of a broker, the license of the broker, associate broker or salesperson shall be automatically terminated upon the issuance of a court order authorizing payment from the Real Estate Recovery Fund. No such licensee shall be eligible to receive a new license until repayment has been made in full, plus interest at the rate prescribed in Section 12-109 of the Code of Civil Procedure, as now or hereafter amended, the amount paid from the Real Estate Recovery Fund on their account. A discharge in bankruptcy shall not relieve a person from the penalties and disabilities provided in this subsection.

(f) If, at any time, the money deposited in the Real Estate Recovery Fund is insufficient to satisfy any duly authorized claim or portion thereof, the Department shall, when sufficient money has been deposited in the Real Estate Recovery Fund, satisfy such unpaid claims or portions thereof, in the order that such claims or portions thereof were originally filed, plus accumulated interest at the rate of prescribed in Section 12-109 of the Code of Civil Procedure, as now or hereafter amended.

SECTION 26. The sums received by the Department pursuant to the provisions of Sections 23 through 30 of this Act shall be deposited into the State Treasury and held in a special fund to be known as the Real Estate Recovery Fund, and except for interest and dividends received from the investment of money in such fund, shall be held by the Department in trust for carrying out the purposes of this Act. These funds may be invested and reinvested in the same manner as funds of the State Employees' Retirement System. All interest and dividends received from investment of funds in the Real Estate Recovery Fund shall be deposited in a special fund in the State Treasury to be known as the Real Estate Research and Education Fund and shall be used only for the ordinary and contingent expenses of operation of the Office of Real Estate Research or its successor, by whatever name designated, at the University of Illinois.

SECTION 27. When the Department receives any process, notice, order or other document provided for or required under this Act, it may enter an appearance, file an answer, appear at the court hearing, defend the action, or take whatever other action it deems appropriate on behalf and in the name of the defendant, and take recourse through any appropriate method of review on behalf of, and in the name of, the defendant.

SECTION 28. When, upon the order of the court, the Department has paid from the Real Estate Recovery Fund any sum to the judgment creditor, the Department shall be subrogated to all of the rights of the judgment creditor and the judgment creditor shall assign all right, title, and interest in the judgment to the Department and any amount and interest so recovered by the Department on the judgment shall be deposited in the Real Estate Recovery Fund.

SECTION 29. The failure of an aggrieved person to comply with this Act relating to the Real Estate Recovery Fund shall constitute a waiver of any rights under Sections 23 through 30 of this Act.

SECTION 30. Nothing contained in Sections 23 through 30 of this Act limits the authority of the Department to take disciplinary action against any licensee for a violation of this Act, or the rules and regulations of the Department; nor shall the repayment in full of all obligations to the Real Estate Recovery Fund by any licensee nullify or modify the effect of any other disciplinary proceeding brought pursuant to this Act.

SECTION 31. The Board shall recommend and the Department approve rules: (1) defining what constitutes a school offering work in subjects relating to real estate transactions which shall include the subjects upon which an applicant is examined in determining fitness to receive a license; (2) providing for the establishment of a uniform and reasonable standard of instruction and maintenance to be observed by such schools; and (3) defining an approved school, college or university, reputable and in good standing.

Every person who desires to operate a real estate school shall make application to the Department in writing in form and substance satisfactory to the Department and pay the required fees prescribed in Section 15 of this Act. The Department may withdraw approval of an approved real estate school or approval of a course offered by a school for good cause.

SECTION 32. Engaging in business as a broker, associate broker or salesperson by any person in violation of this Act is declared to be harmful to the public welfare and to be a public nuisance. An action to enjoin any person from such unlawful activity may be maintained in the name of the People of the State of Illinois by the Attorney General, by the State's Attorney of the county in which the action is brought, by the Department, or by any resident citizen. This remedy shall be in addition to other remedies provided for violation of this Act.

1983 and promulgated pursuant to the Act repealed herein shall remain in full force and effect on the effective date of this Act without being promulgated again by the Department, except to the extent any such rule or regulation is inconsistent with any provision of this Act.

[NOTE: **Sections 36 and 37 of the Illinois Real Estate License Law of 1983 make appropriate changes in other Illinois Statutes which reference the Illinois Real Estate License Law.]**

SECTION 38. "The Real Estate Brokers and Salesmen License Act", approved September 20, 1973, as amended, is repealed.

SECTION 39. This Act takes effect January 1, 1984.

SECTION 33. It is declared to be the public policy of this State, pursuant to paragraphs (h) and (i) of Section 6 of Article VII of the Illinois Constitution of 1970, that any power or function set forth in this Act to be exercised by the State is an exclusive State power or function. Such power or function shall not be exercised concurrently, either directly or indirectly, by any unit of local government, including home rule units, except as otherwise provided in this Act.

Nothing in this Section shall be construed to affect or impair the validity of Section 11-11.1-1 of the Illinois Municipal Code, as amended, or to deny to the corporate authorities of any municipality the powers granted in that Act to enact ordinances: prescribing fair housing practices, defining unfair housing practices, establishing Fair Housing or Human Relations Commissions and standards for the operation of such commissions in the administration and enforcement of such ordinances; prohibiting discrimination based on race, color, creed, ancestry, national origin or physical or mental handicap in the listing, sale, assignment, exchange, transfer, lease, rental or financing of real property for the purpose of the residential occupancy thereof; and prescribing penalties for violations of such ordinances.

SECTION 34. The Illinois Administrative Procedure Act is hereby expressly adopted and incorporated herein as if all of the provisions of such Act were included in this Act, except that the provision of paragraph (c) of Section 16 of The Illinois Administrative Procedure Act, which provides that at hearings the licensee has the right to show compliance with all lawful requirements for retention, or continuation or renewal of the license, is specifically excluded, and for the purposes of this Act the notice required under Section 10 of The Administrative Procedure Act is deemed sufficient when mailed to the last known address of a party.

SECTION 35. All certificates and licenses in effect on December 31, 1983 and issued pursuant to the Act repealed herein are reinstated for the balance of the term for which last issued. All rules and regulations in effect on December 31,

Index

A

Adverse possession, 46
Advertising
    broker, 78, 80-81
    financing terms in, 80
    owner's permission for, 80-81
    rental finding service, 67-69
    salesperson, 80
    truth in, 80
Age
    and contracts, 40-41
    of license applicants, 69
    tax exemptions for, 32, 33
Assessments
    equalization factor in, 31
    homestead tax concessions on, 32-33
    increase in, 32
    mobile home, 34-35
    personal property exemption on, 34-35
    sold-property, 53
    special, 35
    tax rate, 31
Associate brokers (see also Brokers; Salespersons)
    licensing of, 65-89

B

Blue Sky Laws, 92
Brokerage, 1-5
Brokers
    advertising by, 78, 80-81
    as Commissioner of Real Estate, 66
    commissions to, 1, 39, 73, 78, 120
    complaints against, 81
    contracts with, 1, 39-44
    contractual limitations of, 42
    corporations as, 71
    fiduciary responsibility of, 2, 7-8
    liability of, 2-3
    licensing of, 65-89
    partnerships as, 71
    penalties for, 81-82
    place of business of, 76
    prosecution of, 81-82
    -salespersons contract, 2
Business offenses, corporations' and partnerships', 81-82

C

Chief of Real Estate Investigations, 84
Civil Rights Act, 109
Closing, 113-125
    prorations in, 113-115
    sample transaction for, 115-121
    settlement statement worksheet for, 116-119, 147
    statements of, 40, 113
    taxes on, 114
    wages in, 114-115
Commissioner of Real Estate, 66
Commissions, 1, 39, 73, 78, 120
Condominium Property Act, 18, 19
Condominiums, 18-19
    declaration of ownership of, 18
    legal description of, 18
    owners' association for, 18-19
    taxes on, 18
Consumer protectionism, 2, 3 (see also Fraud)
Contracts, 1, 39-44
    changes in, 39
    chattels in, 41
    farm property, 41
    guaranteed sales plan, 7, 79-80

    holiday-executed, 41
    installment, 41-42
    limitations of brokers in making, 42
    "Offer-to-Purchase," 39
    personal property in, 41
    with minors, 40-41
Co-ownership, 15
    partition of, 16
Corporations
    as brokers, 71, 81-82
    as owners, 16, 47
    business offenses by, 81-82
    shares in, 92
Curtesy, abolishment of, 11, 45

D

Deeds
    foreign-language, 60
    grant, bargain, and sale, 47
    holiday-executed, 41
    in trust, 16
    notary acknowledgment of signatures on, 60-61
    of conveyance, 15
    preparation of, 121
    quitclaim, 47
    Recorder of, 59
    recording, 47, 120
    requirements for, 46-47
    trust, 91-92
    warranty, 47
Descent, Laws of, 17, 45, 46
Development, property, 103-104
Disability, tax exemption for, 32
Disciplinary hearings, 81
Disclosure
    of material facts, 7-8
    of special compensation, 8
Discrimination, 107-111
    in listing agreements, 7, 109
Dower, abolishment of, 11, 45

E

Earnest money, 40, 113, 119
Easements, prescriptive, 11
Educational Testing Service, 71-72, 74, 127, 128
Enabling acts, 103-104
Equal opportunity (see Discrimination)
Escheat, 11
Escrow accounts, 40, 91-92
    closing in, 115
Estates in land, 11-13

Ethical practices, 107-111
ETS (see Educational Testing Service)
Eviction, 99
Examination, license, 71-72, 127-146
    broker's, 131
    legal questions in, 127
    preparation for, 131
    salesperson's, 128-131
    sample, 128-131, 132-146
    special fields in, 128
    tips on, 132
Exemptions, tax
    age, 32
    airport land, 33
    disability, 32
    improvement, 33
    increased assessment, 32
    maintenance and repair, 33
    senior citizen, 33
    solar heating, 33
    title transfer, 48

F

Fair housing laws, 107-111
    local, 109
Federal Fair Housing Act, 109
Financing, 91-95, 119, 127-128
    mortgage, 80, 91
Fines, brokers' and salespersons', 82
"Four unities" practice, 15
Fraud, 2-3, 40 (see also Consumer protectionism; Misrepresentation)
    penalties for, 77-79
    Statute of, 40

G

Government powers, 11
Green sheet, 48, 50-52, 59
G.R.I. designation, 3

H

Holiday transactions, 41
Home rule, 103
Homestead exemption, 12
    for taxes, 32-33
Homestead rights, waiver of, 12, 47

I

Illinois Business Corporation Act, 16
Illinois Consumer Fraud and Deceptive Practices Act, 2-3

Illinois Human Rights Act, 79, 107-108
Illinois Land Registration Act, 59, 60, 128
Illinois Land Sales Act, 103-104
Illinois Law of Descent and Distribution, 45
Illinois Plat Act, 26, 59
Illinois Real Estate License Act, 1, 39, 65, 107, 113, 128, 153-172
    administration of, 65-66
    exemptions from 67
    violations of, 81-84
    prosecution and penalties under, 81-82
Illinois Real Estate Transfer Tax Act, 48
Illinois Statute of Frauds, 40
Improvements, tax exemptions for, 33
Inheritance, 45 (see also Wills)
Insurance
    condominium, 19
    fire and hazard, 120-121
    title, 120

J

Judgments, 36

L

Land trusts
    beneficiary of, 17
    benefits of, 17-18
    time limit in, 17
Laws of Descent, 17, 45, 46
Leases, 97-102
    code violations and, 97
    default in, 99
    expiration of, 98-99
    liability in, 97
    recording, 97
    rent concessions in, 98
    security deposits for, 98
    termination of, 98-99
Legal descriptions, land, 18, 23-29
License laws
    administration of, 65-66
    exemptions from, 67
Licenses, brokers', associate brokers', and salespersons', 65-89
    application for, 71, 72
    corporation, 71
    disciplinary hearings on, 81
    examination for, 71-72, 127-146
    expiration of, 74

    fees for, 74-76
        renewal, 74, 75
    inactive, 70, 75
    nonresident, 73-74
    partnership, 71
    refusal of, 76-79
    reinstatement of, 75
    renewal of, 74, 75
    revocation of, 76-79, 83
    suspension of, 76-79
Liens (see also Taxes)
    general, 36
    mechanic's 35-36
    notice of, 35
    right of, 35-36
    waivers of, 36
Listing agreements, 1, 7-9 (see also Contracts)
    changes in, 7, 39
    commission in, 7
    description of property in, 7
    discrimination in, 7, 109
    earnest money deposit in, 7
    exclusive, 7
    expiration date in, 7
    guaranteed sale, 7, 79-80
    list price in, 7
    material facts in, 7-8
    net, 7
    special compensation in, 8, 79
    written, 7

M

Meridian map, 24
Metes and bounds, 23
Misrepresentation, 2
    in advertising, 80
    negligent, 3
    penalties for, 77
Mobile homes, 34-35
Mortgages
    assumed, 114, 119
    financing terms for, 80, 91
    foreclosure and redemption of, 92
    purchase money, 120
    recording, 59
    taxes and, 49

N

Negligence
    broker, 3
    lessor, 97
Notary public, 60-61

O

"Offer-to-Purchase" forms, 39
Ownership
    condominium, 18-19
    corporate, 16, 47
    forms of, 15-22
    in severalty, 15, 16
    intestate, 45
    joint tenancy, 15
    partnership, 16
    tenancy in common, 15-16, 19
    trust, 16-18
Ownership interests (see Estates in land)

P

Partition suits, 16, 18
Partnerships, 16, 18
    as brokers, 71, 81-82
    business offenses by, 81-82
    shares in, 92
Personal property, 41 (see also Mobile homes)
Plat of subdivision, 25, 26
Pocket cards, 72
    fees for duplicate, 76
Principal-agent relationship, 1, 2
    fiduciary duty in, 2, 7-8
Probate, 46
Prorations, 113-115
    computing, 114
Purchase price, 119

R

Real Estate License Administration Fund, 84
Real Estate Recovery Fund, 72, 82, 83-84
    fees for, 75, 83
    management of, 83
    recovery from, 83-84
Real Estate Research and Education Fund, 72, 84
    fees for, 75
Recapitulation, settlement, 122
Rectangular Survey System, federal, 23
Registrar of Titles, 60
Rental finding services, 67-69
    advertising by, 69
    contracts with, 68
    disclosure by, 68-69
    violations of regulations by, 69

S

Sales, public, 16
Salespersons
    advertising by, 80
    -brokers contract, 2
    licensing of, 65-89
    penalties for, 81-82
    prosecution of, 81-82
Scavenger sales, 34
Securities
    prospectus for sales of, 92-93
    registration of, 92-93
Settlement statement worksheet, 116-119, 147
Signs, advertising, 80-81
Sponsor cards, 72-73
    fees for duplicate, 76
Subdivision, 103-104
    Plat of, 25, 26
    registration of, 104
Surveys, land, 23
Survivorship, right of, 15, 45

T

Tax sales, 34
    redemption of, 34
Taxes
    calculation of, 31, 48, 49
    closing, 114
    condominium, 18
    due dates for, 31, 33-34, 120
    estate, 46
    general real estate, 31-32
    homestead exemptions from, 32-33
    Illinois state and county
        transfer, 48
        formula for, 48
        stamp calculation for, 49
    inheritance, 45, 46
    mobile home, 34-35
    municipal transfer, 49
    reserve funds for, 91-92
    senior citizen entitlement for, 33
    title transfer, 48-49, 121
Tenancy (see also Leases)
    farm, 99
    in common, 15-16, 19
    joint, 15
    termination of, 98-99
Title records, 59-63

   acknowledgment of, 60-61
   Torrens System, 36, 59, 60
Title transfer, 45-57
  adverse possession and, 46
  declaration of, 48, 50-52, 59
  Laws of Descent in, 17, 45, 46
  tax on, 48-49, 121
   Illinois state and county, 49
   municipal, 49
Titles, fee simple, 18, 47
Torrens System, 36, 59, 60
Trusts
  land, 16-18
  living, 16
  testamentary, 16

U

Uniform Partnership Act, 16
Uniform Vendor and Purchaser Risk Act, 40

U.S. Geological Survey datum, 26
Usury, 91

V

Valuation, 127-128 (see also Assessments)

W

Wages, building employee, 114-115
Wills, 45, 46
  renunciation of, 46

Z

Zoning, 103-104

REAL ESTATE EDUCATION COMPANY

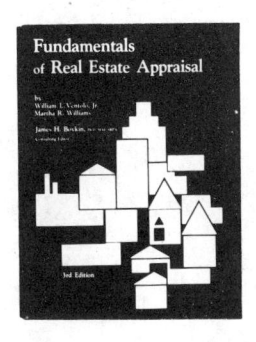

GUIDE TO PASSING THE REAL ESTATE EXAM
By Lawrence Sager

Guide to Passing the Real Estate Exam is the only manual designed specifically for the ACT salesperson and broker exams. Provides additional test-taking drills . . . helps you review important topics . . . and gives the additional confidence you need to pass the ACT real estate exam.

This ACT-style exam manual features . . .
- point-by-point outlines in sections corresponding to the four topic areas of the exam—real estate law, valuation, finance, and special fields
- alphabetical glossary
- diagnostic tests that aid you when identifying areas that require additional study
- hundreds of ACT-style practice questions
- one sample sales and one sample broker exam—both with the answers fully explained
- math review
- section on exam strategies—how to prepare mentally and physically—how to follow directions . . . how to develop a strategy for studying . . . and how to guess

Check box #1 on the order card $14.95   order number 1970-02

FUNDAMENTALS OF REAL ESTATE APPRAISAL, 3rd edition
By William L. Ventolo, Jr. and Martha R. Williams. James Boykin, Consulting Editor

Thorough and concise explanation of real estate appraisal. Covers—in detail—the cost approach . . . market comparison approach . . . and income approach to appraising. NEW TO THIS EDITION . . .
- information on the ways financing techniques affect appraised value—provides numerous examples to give a hands-on feel for this critical element in current appraisals
- section on solar heating added to aid understanding of this form of developing technology as it relates to an appraiser's everyday work
- complete, up-to-date discussion of zoning and depreciation and the way each affects a parcel's value

Numbers and figures have been updated throughout the text to reflect current costs and values of real estate. Features end-of-chapter exams plus glossaries of appraisal and construction terms.

Check box #2 on the order card $28.95   order number 1556-10

ESSENTIALS OF REAL ESTATE FINANCE, 3rd edition
By David Sirota

Popular real estate finance book includes current, up-to-date information—text has been completely revised to include complete coverage of financing methods and instruments in use today. Includes comprehensive discussion of the sources and techniques of financing. Book is clearly written and well organized, while workbook format encourages note-taking.

Special features of the third edition of *Essentials of Real Estate Finance* include . . .
- text revised to reflect changes in laws—you won't have to search for up-to-date information to use . . . Everything you need is included!
- over 50 graphs, charts and tables have been completely updated—emphasize basic principles and apply them to current market conditions
- sample forms and contracts have been incorporated into the appropriate sections for easy reference
- glossary of real estate terms included for quick review

Check box #3 on the order card $28.95   order number 1557-10

Introducing
The Competitive Edge Book Program
from Real Estate Education Company

SPECIAL FREE BOOK

Call or write for your no-obligation free copy.

As a new member of the real estate profession, you are eligible to become a charter member of our Competitive Edge Book Program and receive all these special benefits:

- free booklet entitled "You and Your Career in Real Estate"
- free subscription for all Real Estate Education Company catalogs
- save 40% on the real estate professional Book-of-the-Month special offer
- increase your sales and commissions through our continuing education programs

You are under no obligation to ever purchase a book.

FILL IN THE COUPON OR CALL – TOLL-FREE (800)621-9621. In Illinois, (800)572-9510.

Name _____
Company _____
Address _____
City/State/Zip _____

15-DAY FREE EXAMINATION ORDER CARD

REAL ESTATE EDUCATION COMPANY
a division of Longman Group USA Inc.

Please send me the books I have indicated. I'll return any books I don't want for a full refund within the 15-day period without further obligation.

Detach, Sign, and Mail in Postage-Paid envelope today!

NAME _____
ADDRESS _____
CITY _____
STATE _____ ZIP _____
TELEPHONE # _____

New And Best-Selling Real Estate Books

	Order #		Price	Total Amount
☐ 1.	1970-02	Guide to Passing the Real Estate Exam (ACT)	$14.95	___
☐ 2.	1556-10	Fundamentals of Real Estate Appraisal, 3rd ed.	$28.95	___
☐ 3.	1557-10	Essentials of Real Estate Finance, 3rd ed.	$28.95	___
☐ 4.	1961-01	The Language of Real Estate, 2nd ed.	$21.95	___
☐ 5.	1512-10	Mastering Real Estate Mathematics, 4th ed.	$17.25	___
☐ 6.	1970-04	Questions & Answers to Help You Pass the Real Estate Exam (ETS), 2nd ed.	$14.95	___
☐ 7.	1559-01	Essentials of Real Estate Investment, 2nd ed.	$27.95	___
☐ 8.	1970-03	How To Prepare for the Texas Real Estate Exam, 3rd ed.	$14.95	___
☐ 9.	1510-01	Modern Real Estate Practice, 9th ed.	$27.95	___
☐ 10.	1510-	License law supplements for Modern Real Estate Practice available for many states. Indicate the state you're interested in _____	$ 8.95	___
☐ 11.	1510-02	Modern Real Estate Practice Study Guide	$ 9.25	___
☐ 12.	1909-01	New Home Sales	$19.95	___
☐ 13.	1907-01	Power Real Estate Listing	$12.95	___
☐ 14.	1907-02	Power Real Estate Selling	$12.95	___
☐ 15.	1512-15	Practical Real Estate Financial Analysis: Using the HP-12C Calculator	$19.95	___
☐ 16.	1551-10	Property Management, 2nd ed.	$28.95	___
☐ 17.	1974-01	Protecting Your Sales Commission: Professional Liability in Real Estate	$24.95	___
☐ 18.	1929-01	Real Estate Advertising	$24.95	___
☐ 19.	1965-01	Real Estate Brokerage: A Success Guide	$29.95	___
☐ 20.	1560-01	Real Estate Law	$29.50	___
☐ 21.	1970-01	The Real Estate Education Company Real Estate Exam Manual, 3rd ed. (ETS)	$14.95	___
☐ 22.	1970-05	Selling Tax Shelter and Real Estate Securities: An Introduction to the New NASD Direct Participation Program License	$14.95	___

Book Total ___

PAYMENT MUST ACCOMPANY ALL ORDERS: (check one)
☐ check or money order (payable to Real Estate Education Company)
☐ charge to my credit card (circle one) VISA or MASTERCARD or AMEX

Account No. _____ Exp. date _____
Signature _____

OR CALL OUR TOLL-FREE ORDERING HOTLINE (800) 621-9621 WITH YOUR CHARGE CARD (Illinois residents please call (800) 572-9510)

IL Res. add 8% Sales Tax ___
Postage/Handling $2.00 + .50 postage for each book ___
TOTAL ___